CIVIL RIGHTS MOVEMENT
1954-1968
We Shall Overcome, Some Day

MITCH YAMASAKI, Ph.D.

 Perspectives on History

HistoryCompass

Boston, Massachusetts

HistoryCompass
www.historycompass.com

ISBN 978-1-932663-20-4 paperback edition

10   9   8   7   6   5   4   3   2

Printed in the United States

Subject Reference Guide:

The Civil Rights Movement 1954–1968 We Shall Overcome, Some Day
Edited and Introduced by Mitch Yamasaki, Ph.D.

Civil Rights Movement — U.S. History
Civil Rights Movement — African American History

CIP data available upon request.

Photo/Illustration Credits:

Cover photo: Thousands assembled to demonstrate during the march from the Washington Monument to the Lincoln Memorial (National Museum of American History)

⬥ Table of Contents ⬥

continued

⟡ Table of Contents ⟡

Introduction

SCHOOL DESEGREGATION

Reverend Joseph DeLaine's students needed a bus. Some of them walked nine miles a day to attend his all-black school in Clarendon County, South Carolina. The county had thirty school buses—all of them used by its white schools. When DeLaine asked the county school board chairman for one school bus, he was told "we ain't got no money to buy a bus for your nigger children."

The inequity was not limited to school buses. In 1950, the county spent $179 a year to educate one white student and $43 a year to educate one black student. The parents of DeLaine's students filed a class-action suit alleging that the county's segregated educational system was unconstitutional. Their suit was eventually combined with four related cases and heard before the United States Supreme Court. In *Brown v. Board of Education of Topeka* (1954), the Supreme Court ruled that segregated schools were unconstitutional and ordered them integrated "with all deliberate speed."

DeLaine paid dearly for this victory. He was fired from the teaching position he had held for ten years. His wife, sister, and niece also lost their jobs. DeLaine's house was burned to the ground while white firemen stood by and watched. His church was set ablaze a short time later. DeLaine could not rebuild his church and home because every bank in the county denied him credit. When he shot back at a drive-by sniper, DeLaine was arrested for felonious assault with a deadly weapon. Meanwhile, the county's delaying tactics insured that none of his students would attend an integrated school. Despite such hardships and disappointments, DeLaine and thousands of other civil rights activists kept their "eyes on the prize" and persevered. Their efforts produced one of the most remarkable social revolutions in America's history.

White Resistance

Big Jim Folsom was elected governor of Alabama in 1954 on a populist platform that promised increased funding for schools, roads, and old-age pensions. Folsom's campaign stressed the shared interests of poor whites and blacks. He disparaged racial divisions, proclaiming that "all men are alike." This was the last election Folsom won.

The *Brown* decision dramatically altered politics in the South. The region became preoccupied with race. Virtually no southern politician could survive without espousing "massive resistance" against desegregation. Almost a hundred southern Congressmen signed a "manifesto" denouncing *Brown* and urging their constituents to defy it. Southern state legislatures enacted laws and constitutional amendments challenging or attempting to bypass *Brown*. In southern elections, candidates competed to occupy the most segregationist position. Folsom, who refused to condemn *Brown,* was quickly voted out of office. Folsom's protege,

George Wallace, was labeled a "racial moderate" by his opponents in the 1958 Alabama gubernatorial election. After his defeat, Wallace told a supporter "they out-niggered me this time, but they will never do it again." Wallace went on to become the best known segregationist in southern politics. As governor, he personally blocked the entrance of black students trying to attend the University of Alabama. At his 1963 inauguration, Wallace shouted "Segregation now! Segregation tomorrow! Segregation forever!"

Southerners resented the *Brown* decision because they saw it as yet another attempt by northerners to impose their beliefs and values on the South. Wounds dating back to the Civil War and the Reconstruction resurfaced. Most opponents of desegregration relied on elected officials to block it. But a militant minority felt obliged to do more. They joined "protective societies" to preserve the "southern way of life." The most prominent of these were the White Citizens' Councils. Their members included physicians, lawyers, businessmen, bankers, judges, governors and congressmen. The Councils used economic reprisals "to make it difficult, if not impossible, for any Negro who advocates desegregration to find and hold a job, get credit, or renew a mortgage." The Ku Klux Klan was less respectable and more violent than the Citizens' Councils. Made up mainly of poor rural whites, the Klan resorted to beatings, shootings and bombings to fight integration. The few southern whites who openly supported integration were subjected to economic reprisals, social ostracism and physical violence. This was enough to keep racial moderates silent. As a result, civil rights activists who tried to integrate the South encountered intransigent public officials and vicious private citizens intent on resisting them with "any means necessary."

MONTGOMERY BUS BOYCOTT

On December 1, 1955, Rosa Parks boarded a bus in Montgomery, Alabama. As required by law, the African American woman took a seat towards the back of the bus. When the bus filled up, the driver ordered Parks to give her seat up to a white passenger. She refused. Authorities arrested Parks for violating the city's transportation ordinance.

That night, black community leaders decided to protest the city's segregated bus system with a one-day boycott. They thought the boycott would be effective because blacks made up the largest segment of Montgomery's bus riders. On December 5, 1955, the day of Rosa Parks' trial, over ninety percent of Montgomery's blacks boycotted the city's buses. Nearly empty buses drove through the city's streets. Exhilarated by its success, organizers decided to continue the boycott until three demands were met: (1) that black passengers be treated courteously, (2) that seating should be on a first-come-first-served basis, (3) that black bus drivers be hired for predominantly black routes.

City leaders refused to consider their demands. Instead, Mayor W.A. Gayle and Montgomery's White Citizens' Council launched a "get-tough" policy. "White people,"

Gayle proclaimed, "do not care whether the Negroes ever ride a city bus again if it means that the social fabric of our community is to be destroyed." The police harassed carpools, organized to drive black domestic workers to their jobs in white sections of Montgomery. Many boycott leaders were fired from their jobs. They also faced arrests and violence. The young clergyman Martin Luther King, Jr. was jailed and his house was bombed. He emerged from the boycott as one of the most influential leaders of the African American civil rights movement.

During the boycott, Gayle was particularly frustrated by white women quietly driving their maids to and from their homes. He published a list of "whites acting as chauffeurs to Negroes boycotting the buses." Women on the list were ostracized by friends and relatives. They also received threatening phone calls. Nevertheless, some of them continued to drive their employees.

Most people thought the bus boycott would last a week or two. It went on for almost a year, ending in November of 1956, when the United States Supreme Court ruled that Montgomery's segregated bus system was unconstitutional. Towards the end of the boycott, an elderly housekeeper was asked how she felt about walking to work everyday. She replied, "My feets is tired but my soul is rested."

SIT-INS

On February 1, 1960, four young men from a nearby black college walked into the Woolworth store in

Greensboro, North Carolina. They sat down at the lunch counter. One of them told a waitress "I'd like a cup of coffee, please." "I'm sorry," she replied, "We don't serve Negroes here." Instead of leaving, Ezell Blair, Jr., Franklin McCain, Joseph McNeil and David Richmond continued to sit. The store manager decided that the best policy was to ignore them. He let the young men sit at the counter until closing time.

Sit-in at F.W. Woolworth's, in Greensboro, NC (UPI)

Next morning, the four returned with students from other black colleges. Most brought their books and studied at the segregated lunch counter. Every once in a while, a student would ask a waitress, "Miss, may I make an order?" The waitresses ignored them. On the third day, the black students were joined by white students from the state women's college. Demonstrators occupied sixty-three of the sixty-six seats at the lunch counter. The Greensboro "sit-in" became a national news event. The sit-ins spread. Within two months, they were taking place in fifty-four cities in nine states.

The sit-ins caused angry reactions in some southern cities. White hecklers taunted black sit-in students and their white sympathizers. Some threw french fries and chewing gum at them. Others poured sugar, milk, catsup and coffee over their heads. On February 27, 1960, white teenagers in Nashville, Tennessee physically assaulted sit-in demonstrators. They pulled demonstrators off their lunch counter stools, then punched and kicked them. None of the demonstrators fought back. When the police arrived, they only arrested the demonstrators, charging them with "disorderly conduct."

Student leaders from southern black colleges held a convention during Easter weekend 1960 to better organize the growing sit-in movement. The convention stressed nonviolence. Organizers told civil rights activists to expect beatings from white agitators and local police. But "don't strike back or curse back if attacked," they insisted. "Remember the teachings of Jesus, Gandhi and Martin Luther King."

At the convention, the students formed the Student Nonviolent Coordinating Committee (SNCC) to facilitate future sit-ins and other forms of demonstrations. Following the advice of veteran civil rights activist Ella Baker, students made SNCC democratic and decentralized. Instead of relying on a charismatic leader, SNCC told its members "if you are looking for a leader, look in the mirror." They did. As SNCC leaders were beaten unconscious or hauled off to jail, a steady stream of SNCC members stepped forward to take their places.

ALBANY AND BIRMINGHAM

After the Montgomery bus boycott, Martin Luther King, Jr. helped establish the Southern Christian Leadership Conference (SCLC) to carry on the civil rights struggle. As SCLC president, King traveled extensively, supporting the efforts of African Americans to integrate their communities. In December of 1961, King's college classmate William Anderson asked him to help the troubled civil rights movement in Albany, Georgia. Albany officials adamantly refused to integrate its schools, parks and other public accommodations. Meanwhile, civil rights organizations, such as the NAACP and SNCC, squabbled over tactics and leadership. King arrived in Albany with no clear plan of action. He encountered Police Chief Laurie Pritchett, who had read King's writings on nonviolent civil disobedience and had formulated a strategy to counter it. When civil rights activists tried to overflow Albany's jails by conducting illegal demonstrations, they found that Pritchett had secured sufficient jail space in adjoining counties. As one demonstrator noted, "We ran out of people before Pritchett ran out of jails." Pritchett made sure that arrests were not tainted by police brutality. He even prayed with protesters before locking them up. When King was arrested, city officials quickly released him, saying that a mysterious benefactor had paid his fines. Pritchett then told the press that hundreds of Albany blacks were languishing in jail while King walked free. He depicted King and the SCLC as "outside agitators" with no long term concern for the city. When King left Albany in August of 1962, Pritchett boasted that the city was "as segregated as ever." King swore off spontaneous rescue missions after Albany, telling his colleagues, "I don't want to be a fireman anymore."

SCLC leaders held a three-day retreat in December of 1962.Albany weighed heavily on their minds. King and his associates desperately wanted to prove that their nonviolent strategy was still viable. They decided to prove this in Birmingham, Alabama. Black newspapers called Birmingham the "worst big city in the U.S.A." Between 1957 and 1963, the bombings of eighteen homes and churches in black neighborhoods went unsolved. In 1962, the city closed all of its public parks, playgrounds and swimming pools rather than comply with a federal court order to integrate them. The city's police commissioner, Theophilus Eugene "Bull" Connor, was a staunch segregationist with a history of brutalizing African Americans. Reverend Fred Shuttlesworth, who invited King to come to Birmingham, had been chain whipped by a white mob in 1957 for trying to enroll his children in an all-white school.

SCLC carefully planned its Birmingham campaign, which was to include marches, boycotts and sit-ins. They called it Project "C"—for confrontation. They hoped to draw national attention to peaceful civil rights demonstrators confronted by the city's brutal police force. But when they launched Project "C" everything went wrong. First, most Birmingham blacks, fearful of being arrested and losing their jobs, chose not to take part in the demonstrations. King could not get more than fifty marchers for any of his demonstrations. Second, black community leaders criticized King for bringing unwanted trouble to the city. Third, white moderates, who helped to defeat "Bull" Connor in the recent mayoral election, were upset at King "because he wouldn't give us a chance to prove what we could do through the political processes." Federal officials agreed. They thought it was counterproductive for SCLC to be agitating in a city where the incoming administration pledged to bring about civil rights reforms. Fourth, Connor exercised remarkable restraint in dealing with demonstrators. As a result, there was virtually no media coverage of the demonstrations. Finally, SCLC ran out of money to bail out the few demonstrators that volunteered to go to jail.

"Look, I don't know what to do," King told his staff, "I just know that something has to change in Birmingham. I don't know whether I can raise money to get people out of jail. I do know that I can go to jail with them." King got himself arrested the next day. In jail, he read and heard about the criticisms lodged against his campaign. King uncharacteristically lashed back at the critics in his "Letter from a Birmingham Jail."

When King came out of jail, nothing had changed. Things looked hopeless. It was at this time that Reverend James Bevel approached him with a radical plan. He suggested using Birmingham's black youngsters in the campaign. King's senior advisers opposed the plan. They told him that no conscientious adult could sacrifice children as "battle fodder." But King had come too far and given too much to let the movement die in Birmingham. After deep contemplation, he decided to place its fate in the hands of school children.

On May 2, 1963, hundreds of children, some as young as six years old, filed out of Birmingham's churches to demonstrate in the streets. In a few days, their numbers swelled into the thousands. Caught off guard, Connor resorted to the brutality that he was known for. He turned high pressure fire hoses and attack dogs on the children. As the police hauled the children into patrol wagons, the demonstrators sang "I ain't scared of your jail, cause I want my freedom." Captured on national television, these events aroused the conscience of millions of Americans. Support for the civil rights movement surged. President John F. Kennedy, who had done virtually nothing to promote civil rights, felt compelled to act. In a powerful televised speech, he called for comprehensive civil rights legislation. On May 7, 1963, city leaders agreed to sit down and negotiate the integration of Birmingham's public facilities.

In the history of the civil rights movement, tragedy often followed success. Sunday, September 15, 1963 was annual Youth Day at Birmingham's Sixteenth Street Baptist Church. In the church basement, four young black girls debated the topic of the sermon they were about to deliver—"The Love That Forgives." Just then, a large explosion rocked the church. Minutes later, school teacher Maxine McNair desperately searched through the rubble of the bombed out church to find her daughter. She came upon an old man who was weeping. "Daddy," she screamed, "I can't find Denise!" "She's dead, baby," he replied, "I've got one of her shoes." The McNairs, along with the families of the other three girls, had to identify their children's bodies at the city morgue. They went home from the morgue in rage and disbelief. That afternoon, black and white strangers came to their door to express their condolences. Some of the distraught whites drove up in cars bearing Confederate license plates.

VOTING RIGHTS STRUGGLE

In the summer of 1962, Fanny Lou Hamer attended a voter registration meeting conducted by Bob Moses of SNCC in Sunflower County, Mississippi. The meeting inspired the forty-four year old sharecropper. Hamer had struggled all her life under a political and economic system that kept blacks down. She volunteered, along with seventeen other blacks, to go to the court house in Indianola to register. At the courthouse, officials ordered the applicants to give their residence, place of employment and other information that was later used to identify and intimidate them. They were then given literacy tests—interpreting parts of the Mississippi Constitution. Officials did not tell the applicants whether they passed the test. As the bus carrying the applicants left Indianola, authorities intercepted it and fined the driver $100 for operating an improperly-colored bus.

When she got home, Hamer was fired from her job and evicted from her home. Hamer later learned that she had failed the literacy test. Undeterred, Hamer returned every thirty days to take the test until she passed it in January 1963. She also helped civil rights activists recruit applicants for voter registration. As a result of these actions, Hamer's husband and daughter lost their jobs. The Hamers received a $9,000 water bill from the county although their house had no running water. Fanny was shot at from a speeding car. She was arrested and beaten in jail.

By the early 1960s, Bob Moses, director of Mississippi's Council of Federal Organizations (COFO), saw voting rights as the most effective means of empowering African Americans. He and other young civil rights activists tied black disenfranchisement to poverty and other forms of deprivation. In Mississippi, where less than five percent of black adults were registered to vote, the median annual income of black families was $1,444, one third that of white families. In Dallas County, Alabama, where only one percent of its black residents were registered voters, their median income was $28 a week. In the neighboring counties of Lowndes and Wilcox, African Americans made up nearly eighty percent of the population but not one of them was registered to vote. Black families in those counties earned a median income of $20 a week.

Voter registration was the most dangerous activity undertaken by civil rights activists. They lived and worked among poor blacks who could not protect them from local authorities or Ku Klux Klansmen. This suited Moses. The Harvard University graduate and high school teacher was shy, soft-spoken and modest. He was also undaunted. With the help of local high school students, Moses went door-to-door trying to get blacks in rural Mississippi to register. He initially convinced a handful of black farmers to register. But when one of them was shot it became nearly impossible to recruit others. COFO workers tried to reassure registrants by driving them to the court house. Highway patrolmen, however, routinely pulled them over for various traffic violations. In town, white mobs waited to physically assault them. When COFO worker John Hardy reported his beating, the county sheriff arrested him for "inciting a riot." "Night riders" riddled the homes of COFO workers with bullets. Their offices were ransacked and burned to the ground. Many COFO workers developed ulcers, migraine headaches, and nervous twitches from the strain. Despite their efforts, between 1962 and 1964, the proportion of black voters in Mississippi only rose from 5.3 percent to 6.7 percent.

In time, Moses realized that civil rights activists had to foster indigenous black leaders in order to carry on a patient, grassroots struggle. Courageous Mississippi residents, such as Fanny Lou Hamer, filled these roles. Moses also believed that they needed federal enforcement to secure voting rights for southern blacks. For this, they needed national exposure. But the grassroots voter registration campaign was invisible outside of a few rural southern communities. Hoping to attract national attention and to temper racist violence, COFO recruited large numbers of white volunteers to work in its Mississippi "Freedom Summer" project. Hundreds of white volunteers, mostly from colleges outside the South, came to Mississippi in the summer of 1964. They helped register black voters and taught in "freedom schools" for local black children.

Many white Mississippians saw the "Freedom Summer" project as an invasion of their state. Some of them resorted to violence. They beat civil rights workers, bombed the homes of cooperating blacks and burned down churches used for COFO meetings. Ku Klux Klansmen murdered three civil rights workers — one black (James Chaney) and two white (Andrew Goodman and Michael Schwerner). But civil rights activists and Mississippians committed to voting rights had come too far to intimidated. They continued the struggle until flagrant brutality of white racists in the deep South moved the nation to call for a federal Voting Rights Act, which Congress enacted in 1965.

BLACK NATIONALISM AND BLACK POWER

"When my mother was pregnant with me...a party of hooded Ku Klux Klan riders galloped up to our home in

Omaha, Nebraska." *The Autobiography of Malcolm X* (1964) opens with these words. The Klansmen came for Malcolm's father, Earl Little, a black preacher who advocated the separatist doctrine of Marcus Garvey. When they found that Little was not home, the Klansmen threatened his wife and children, then rode off. Little moved his family to Lansing, Michigan shortly after Malcolm was born on May 19, 1925. In Lansing, Little ran afoul of The Black Legion, a local white racist society. The Legionnaires saw Little as an "uppity nigger" trying to spread "unrest and dissension" among the community's "good niggers." One night in 1929, Malcolm was "snatched awake into a frightening confusion of pistol shots and shouting and smoke and flames." Malcolm's father shot at the white men who had set fire to their home while the rest of the family scrambled to get out. When Malcolm was six years old, his father was killed in Lansing under suspicious circumstances. His mother tried to maintain the large household by herself. But the strains were too much. She suffered a nervous breakdown and was committed to a mental institution in 1937. The state sent Malcolm and the other children to relatives and foster homes.

Malcolm Little attended integrated schools in East Lansing, Michigan, where he was the only black student in his eighth grade class. This, however, did not prevent his excelling in school and being selected class valedictorian. Malcolm looked up to his eighth grade English teacher, whom he thought of as a mentor. One day, that teacher asked him what he wanted to become. Malcolm told him "I've been thinking I'd like to be a lawyer." "A lawyer," the teacher replied. "That's no realistic goal for a nigger." Malcolm knew that the teacher was trying to shield him from disappointment. This made the experience all the more painful. Disillusioned and left mostly unsupervised, Malcolm became a street hoodlum in Boston and New York. In 1946, Boston police arrested Malcolm for burglary. He received a long prison sentence mainly because his accomplices included two white females. In prison, Malcolm taught himself to read and write. He also discovered the Nation of Islam. He immediately joined the Nation after being released from prison in 1952. Malcolm received his "X," symbolizing "the true African family name that he never could know." In 1954, Malcolm X became minister of the Nation's Temple Number Seven in Harlem, New York.

Malcolm X's life shows that racism in the United States was not confined to the South. The fact that segregation laws existed only in the South reflected demographics rather than attitudes. Before the twentieth century, ninety percent of African Americans lived in the South. Between 1910 and 1970, six and a half million blacks migrated out of the South. Some headed west. But most of them moved to northern cities such as Chicago, New York and Philadelphia. By 1970, forty-five percent of the blacks lived outside the South. At the same time, the black population became more urban. In 1910, only twenty-five percent of blacks lived in cities. By 1970, sixty-nine percent of blacks resided in metropolitan areas. Like other immigrants, African Americans moving to cities settled in their own ethnic ghettoes. In other words, prior to the twentieth century, so few blacks lived outside the South that their presence posed little concern to the predominantly white communities in which they lived. Whites outside the South did not see any need for segregation laws in the twentieth century because most blacks in their region lived in black ghettoes. White communities in the North and the West tried to maintain this *de facto* segregation by requiring home buyers to sign covenants pledging that they would not sell their homes to blacks. Prejudice against blacks extended beyond housing. Most northern unions excluded blacks from membership. This meant that most blacks could not obtain the high paying blue collar jobs in northern industries. In his autobiography, Malcolm X remarked that the best job a black man could hope for in New York City before World War II was to be a doorman at the Ritz Hotel. When Martin Luther King, Jr. tried to bring SCLC's brand of nonviolent civil rights agitation north to Chicago in 1965, he met stiff and often violent resistance from the city's white population. One of the most bitter battles over the busing of students to bring about integration was fought in Boston, birthplace of the *ante bellum* Abolitionist Movement.

For blacks outside the South, civil rights did not mean challenging segregation laws. It meant better jobs, decent housing and adequate social services. Conditions for blacks in the inner cities deteriorated after World War II with the migration of whites to the suburbs. Those left behind, many of them poor blacks, faced disappearing jobs, declining public services, decaying infrastructures and rising crime rates. At the beginning of the 1960s, more than half of African Americans lived in poverty. Black unemployment doubled that of whites. Blacks were twice as likely to be victimized by crime than whites.

Black ghettoes in America's cities exploded in the 1960s. The first major riot occurred in the Watts section of Los Angeles in the summer of 1965. During a routine traffic citation, a white police officer struck a protesting black bystander with his club. This seemingly minor incident unleashed the pent up bitterness and frustrations of Watts' black population. Upwards of 10,000 rioters attacked white motorists, looted stores, burned buildings and sniped at firemen and policemen. National Guardsmen were called in to squelch the riot. The riot resulted in 34 deaths, 28 of them black, and millions of dollars in property damage. Forty-three more ghetto riots swept across the nation in the summer of 1966. Eight more major riots broke out during the following summer. The most serious of these, in Detroit, left 43 people dead, 33 of them black.

Many urban blacks rejected the notion of peacefully integrating with whites. A few of them turned to the nationalist/separatist doctrine of the Nation of Islam. The Nation urged blacks to practice self-discipline and self-respect. It also exhorted African Americans to separate themselves from the "white devils." The message of its most eloquent spokesman, Malcolm X, reached far beyond the Nation's membership. He told African Americans to be proud of their blackness and their African roots. He also maintained that blacks must take control their own destinies "by any means necessary."

Malcolm X was murdered in 1965 by rivals within the Nation of Islam after he broke with its leader Elijah Muhammed. Nevertheless, his ideas influenced the growth of "black power." As a doctrine, black power meant different things to different groups. To some blacks, it meant affirming their Afro-American heritage through their food, clothing, hair style, literature and music. To others, such as the Black Panthers, it meant creating segregated and armed black communities. In all its manifestations, however, black power represented a shift away from efforts to integrate towards an awareness of racial distinctiveness.

Sources

Brown v. Board of Education

Brown v. Board of Education of Topeka (1954) *was actually five cases heard together on appeal before the United States Supreme Court. The National Association for the Advancement of Colored People (NAACP) represented the plaintiff in each case. It alleged that the segregated educational institutions named in Brown violated the Fourteenth Amendment to the United States Constitution (ratified in 1868), which mandated that "no state shall... deny any person within its jurisdiction the equal protection of the laws." The greatest hurdle that the NAACP faced was the "separate but equal" doctrine established in Plessy v. Ferguson (1896). This doctrine permitted states to maintain segregated public schools, despite the Fourteenth Amendment's "equal protection" mandate, provided that the schools dispensed "equal education." In earlier cases, the NAACP'S legal defense team, led by Charles Houston and Thurgood Marshall, sued educational institutions that failed to provide equal education to black students. But in Brown it argued that all segregated schools were unequal because segregation was inherently incompatible with equal education. The Supreme Court agreed with the NAACP in its unanimous opinion:*

> Does segregation of children in public schools solely on the basis of race, even though the physical

facilities and other "tangible" factors may be equal, deprive children of the minority group of equal educational opportunities? We believe it does....

To separate them from others of similar age and qualifications solely because of their race generates a feeling of inferiority as to their status in the community that may affect their hearts and minds in a way very unlikely to ever be undone....

We conclude that in the field of public education the doctrine of "separate but equal" has no place. Separate educational facilities are inherently unequal.

Source: 175 U.S. 528; *reprinted in* Waldo Martin, *Brown v. Board of Education: A Brief History with Documents* (Boston: Bedford, 1998), pp. 173-74.

The Supreme Court heard arguments for implementing Brown at a subsequent session. Southern officials, noting the diversity of their urban and rural school districts, argued for gradual integration. The NAACP argued that a clear deadline was necessary to prevent "foot dragging." The Supreme Court felt that it was not appropriate to set a national deadline. Instead, it ordered that school desegregation proceed "with all deliberate speed." Supervision of the desegregation process was left to federal district courts.

Most border states, with tiny black populations, complied quickly. By 1956, seventy percent of their school districts operated biracial schools. But states in the deep

South, with large black populations, waged "massive resistance" campaigns against desegregation. Ten years after Brown, fewer than one percent of black students in the deep South attended integrated schools. It was not until the 1970s, when passions had died down and the enticement of federal aid to schools (conditioned on desegregation) became irresistible, that the majority of black students in the deep South began attending integrated schools.

Southern Manifesto

The Brown decision produced a backlash among southern politicians. This was expressed in the so-called "Southern Manifesto" (1956), signed by ninety-six southern Congressmen:

> We regard the decision of the Supreme Court in the school cases as a clear abuse of judicial power. It climaxes a trend in the Federal judiciary undertaking to legislate in derogation of the authority of Congress, and to encroach upon the reserved rights of the States and the people....
>
> This unwarranted exercise of power by the Court, contrary to the Constitution, is creating chaos and confusion in the States principally affected. It is destroying amicable relations between the white and Negro races that have been created through 90 years of patient effort by the good people of both races. It

has planted hatred and suspicion where there has been heretofore friendship and understanding.

Without regard to the consent of the governed, outside agitators are threatening immediate and revolutionary changes in our public-school systems. If done, this is certain to destroy the system of public education in some of the States....

We commend the motives of those States which have declared the intention to resist forced integration by any lawful means....

Even though we constitute a minority in the present Congress, we have full faith that a majority of the American people believe in the dual system of Government which has enabled us to achieve our greatness and will in time demand that the reserved rights of the States and of the people be made secure against judicial usurpation.

We pledge ourselves to use all lawful means to bring about a reversal of this decision which is contrary to the Constitution and to prevent the use of force in its implementation.

In this trying period, as we all seek to right this wrong, we appeal to our people not to be provoked by the agitators and troublemakers invading our States and to scrupulously refrain from disorder and lawless acts.

Source: Martin, pp. 220-23.

Fear of Miscegenation

Central to the South's opposition to school integration was the fear of miscegenation. In his article "Mixed Schools and Mixed Blood" (1956), naturalist and historian Herbert Ravenel Sass argued that racial purity had made the United States strong and prosperous:

What may well be the most important physical fact in the story of the United States is one which is seldom emphasized in our history books. It is the fact that throughout the three and a half centuries of our existence we have kept our several races biologically distinct and separate....

The fact that the United States is overwhelmingly pure white is not only important; it is also the most distinctive fact about this country when considered in relation to the rest of the New World.... In general the pure-blooded white nations have out-stripped the far more numerous American mixed-blood nations in most of the achievements which constitute progress as commonly defined....

It is the deep conviction of nearly all white Southerners in the states which have large Negro populations that the mingling or integration of white and Negro children in the South's primary schools would open the gates to miscegenation and widespread racial amalgamation.

This belief is at the heart of our race problem, and until it is realized that this is the South's basic and compelling motive, there can be no understanding of the South's attitude.

Sass maintained that his views on race were supported by science:

Though everywhere else in Nature (as well as in all our plant breeding and animal breeding) race and heredity are recognized as of primary importance, we are told that in the human species race is of no importance and racial differences are due not to heredity but to environment. Science has proved, so we are told, that all races are equal and, in essentials, identical.

Science has most certainly not proved that all races are equal, much less identical; and, as the courageous geneticist, Dr. W.C. George of the University of North Carolina, has recently pointed out, there is overwhelming likelihood that the biological consequences of white and Negro integration in the South would be harmful....

Source: William Dudley, ed., *The Civil Rights Movement: Opposing Viewpoints* (San Diego: Greenhaven Press, 1966), pp. 74-75, 80.

✳ ✳ ✳

Handbills that Helped Organize the Boycott

On the night of Rosa Park's arrest, Jo Ann Robinson met with the Women's Political Council. This organization was formed in Montgomery in 1946, after dozens of African Americans were arrested for violating the city's bus code. Its leaders urged Robinson to initiate a boycott in support of Parks.

Robinson went to Alabama State College, where she taught, and mimeographed 35,000 handbills. She stayed up all night mimeographing. In the morning, Robinson and a few of her students distributed these handbills within the city's black community. These handbills were crucial to the success of the bus boycott.

This is for Monday, December 5, 1955

Another Negro woman has been arrested and thrown in jail because she refused to get up out of her seat on the bus and give it to a white person....

...This has to be stopped.

Negroes have rights, too, for if Negroes did not ride the buses, they could not operate. Three-fourths of the riders are Negroes, yet we are arrested, or have to stand over empty seats. If we do not do something to stop these arrests, they will continue. The next time it may be you, or your daughter, or mother.

This woman's case will come up on Monday. We are, therefore, asking every Negro to stay off the buses Monday in protest of the arrest and trial. Don't ride the buses to work, to town, to school, or anywhere on Monday.

You can afford to stay out of school for one day if you have no other way to go except by bus.

You can also afford to stay out of town for one day. If you work, take a cab, or walk. But please, children and grown-ups, don't ride the bus at all on Monday....

Source: Juan Williams, *Eyes on the Prize: America's Civil Rights Years, 1954-1965* (New York: Penguin Books, 1988), p. 68.

✳✳✳

White Supporters of the Montgomery Bus Boycott

Virginia Foster Durr and her husband, attorney Clifford Durr, openly supported the Montgomery bus boycott. In an interview for the film series Eyes on the Prize, Durr described the consequences whites like themselves faced. The interview also reveals the personal nature of relationships in the South:

The first thing that happened to whites like us who were sympathetic to the boycott was that we lost our businesses. People didn't come to us. We got a reputation. My husband got mighty little law business after he took a very decided stand. People like my husband and Aubrey Williams [publisher of the *Southern Farmer*] realized that they were cutting their own throats. Aubrey lost all of his advertising, every bit of it.

The fact that our family stood by us even though they did not agree with us was our salvation. If they had disowned us, had not stood by us, we could not have stayed. We were lucky because Clifford was kin to so many people in Montgomery County. It was difficult for them to ostracize us on account of that strong feeling of kinship....

There was another kind of terror. Some whites were scared that they wouldn't be invited to the ball, to the parties. It's a terror of being a social failure, of not making your way in the world.

Source: Williams, pp. 82-83.

Black Churches and the Boycott

What was supposed to be a one-day boycott went on for almost a year. The decision to extend the boycott was made in Montgomery's black churches. Weekly church meetings also helped sustain the spirit of the city's black community as they endured the hardships of carrying out the boycott. Reporter Joe Azbell recalled the energy he witnessed at a meeting in the Holt Street Baptist Church:

I came down the street and I couldn't believe there were that many cars. I parked many blocks from the church just to get a place for my car. I went on up to the church, and they made way for me because I was the first white person there...I was two minutes late and they were [already] preaching, and the audience was so on fire that the preacher would get up and say, 'Do you want your freedom?' And they'd say, 'Yeah, I want my freedom!' [The preacher would say,] 'Are you for what we're doing?'; 'Yeah, go ahead, go ahead!'...and they were so excited...I've never heard singing like that...they were on fire for freedom. There was a spirit there that no one could capture again...it was so powerful.

Source: Williams, p. 74.

The Little Rock Nine

On the morning of September 3, 1957, fifteen year old Elizabeth Eckford walked up the steps of Central High School in Little Rock, Arkansas. She was one of nine black students slated to integrate the school. National Guardsmen, however, stopped Eckford and did not let her enter the school. As she left the school, Eckford got separated from the other black students. She was quickly surrounded by an angry white mob numbering in the hundreds. They taunted and threatened her. Someone yelled, "Get her, get the nigger....Hang her!" Eckford walked slowly towards a bus stop bench. As she did, Eckford "tried to see a friendly face somewhere in the mob...looked into the face of an old woman and it seemed a kind face, but when I looked at her again, she spat on me." Eckford was eventually rescued by a white woman who escorted her home on a city bus.

That night, Melba Pattillo, another of the nine blackstudents, made the following diary entry:

> I was disappointed not to see what is inside Central High School.
>
> I don't understand why the governor [Orval Faubus] sent grown-up soldiers to keep us out. I don't know if I should go back.
>
> But Grandma is right, if I don't go back, they will think they have won. They will think they can use soldiers to frighten us, and we'll always have to obey them. They'll always be in charge if I don't go back to Central and make the integration happen.

Governor Faubus brought on the confrontation because he faced a difficult reelection fight in 1958. He understood the political climate that was sweeping through the South. By sending the National Guardsmen to block the integration of Central High, Faubus preempted his segregationist opponents.

The black students sued the governor to prevent him from interfering with the integration of Central High. Their case was heard by the Federal District Court at Little Rock on September 20, 1957. Several of the black students were called to testify in the case. Melba Pattillo Beals describes the courtroom scene:

> "Niggers stink. The room smells now," a voice called out from somewhere behind us. I turned around to see three white ladies directly behind me.

"I'll bet you don't even know your ABC's, monkeys," one of them said. "You monkeys. What are you looking at?" I glowered at her, trying not to say what I was really thinking. Where I came from adults didn't behave that way.

Elizabeth Eckford, being followed by screaming white students in Arkansas.

When the judge announced that the court-ordered integration of Central High School should proceed and that the governor should take no steps to prevent it, someone shouted "Oh, damn nigger-loving judge!" The black students returned to Central High on September 23, 1957. They heard the white mob outside shouting "get the niggers" and "two, four, six, eight, we ain't gonna integrate!" Suddenly, the black students were summoned to the principal's office:

As I followed [my teacher] through an inner office past very official-looking white men, I was alarmed by the anxious expressions on their faces....I heard their frantic tone of voice, heard them say the mob was out of control, that they would have to call for help. "What are we gonna do about the nigger children?" asked one.

"The crowd is moving fast. They've broken the barricades. These kids are trapped in here."

"Good Lord, you're right," another voice said. "We may have to let the mob have one of these kids, so's we can distract them long enough to get the others out."

"Let one of those kids hang? How's that gonna look? Niggers or not, they're children, and we got a job to do."...

"It may be the only way out. There must be a thousand people out there, armed and coming this way."...

I heard footsteps coming closer....

A tall, raw-boned, dark-haired man came toward us. "I'm Gene Smith, Assistant Chief of the Little Rock Police Department." He spoke in a calm tone. "It's time for you to leave for today. Come with me, now." Right away, I had a good feeling about him because of the way he introduced himself and took charge. He urged us to move faster, acting as though it mattered to him whether or not we got out.

While no one was hurt that day, it convinced some parents, including Beals' father, that their children should not be involved with school integration:

Daddy came storming in, huffing and puffing his anger.... Grandma came rushing back from the kitchen to stand in the doorway. He looked at her with angry eyes, pointing his finger at me and shouting in harsh tones that made my knees shake.

"Sacrificing this child's life and endangering the lives and jobs of kinfolks ain't got nothing to do with freedom! We ain't free if we're hungry, or worse yet, hanging from a tree."

"Shut your mouth, Will Pattillo! Don't make this child doubt her good deed," Grandma shouted back. That was just the beginning of an awful string of mean words Papa and Grandma exchanged about me and the integration. The only good thing about his visit was that he hugged me good-bye.

President Dwight D. Eisenhower did not support court-ordered school integration. He thought the Brown decision was a "mistake." "You cannot," Eisenhower stated, "change people's hearts merely by laws." But Faubus' action directly challenged federal authority. It could not be ignored. Nor could Eisenhower permit the lynching of black students. He therefore federalized Arkansas' National Guard and sent elements of the 101st

Airborne Division to Little Rock on September 24, 1957. These soldiers escorted the black students to and from school. They also protected the students in the school. A soldier named Danny accompanied Beals from class to class:

As I walked through the crowded spaces, I felt almost singed by their hostile words and glares. Occasionally students moved in close to elbow me in my side or shove me. That's when Danny would step closer to make certain they saw him. When one boy walked up to try to push me down the stairs, Danny stared him down. The boy backed away, but he shouted at Danny, "Are you proud of protecting a nigger?"...

✳ ✳ ✳

I walked down the steps to where the class would be playing volleyball and joined the others as they divided themselves into teams. But before we could start playing, a girl called out to Danny.

"You like protecting nigger bitches?" She smiled sweetly and fluttered her eyelashes at him. "Wouldn't you rather be following me around instead of her?"

Later, as Beals walked down the hall, she again ran into trouble:

"Hey, Melba, pay attention to what you're doing. Watch out!" Danny shouted as a group of boys bumped straight into me. One of them kicked me in the shins so hard I fell to the floor. A second kick was delivered to my stomach. Danny stood over me, motioning them to move away. Other soldiers made their presence known, although they kept their distance. I struggled to my feet. More white students gathered around and taunted me, applauding and cheering: 'The nigger's down."

"Stand tall," Danny whispered, "Let's move out."

"Why didn't you do something?" I asked him.

"I'm here for one thing," he said impatiently. "To keep you alive. I'm not allowed to get into verbal or physical battles with these students."

After a few days, Beals noticed some positive changes. She made the following optimistic diary entry on September 30, 1957:

A girl smiled at me today, another gave me directions, still another boy whispered the page I should turn to in our textbook. This is going to work. It will take a lot more patience and more strength from me, but it's going to work. It takes more time than I thought. But we're going to have integration in Little Rock.

Not long before the end of the school day, I entered a dimly lit rest room. The three girls standing near the door seemed to ignore me. Their passive, silent, almost pleasant greeting made me uncomfortable, and the more I thought about their attitude, the more it concerned me. At least when students were treating me harshly, I know what to expect.

Once inside the stall, I was even more alarmed at all the movement, the feet shuffling, the voices whispering. It sounded as though more people were entering the room.

"Bombs away!" someone shouted above me. I looked up to see a flaming paper wad coming right down on me. Girls were leaning over the top of the stalls on either side of me. Flaming paper floated down and landed on my hair and shoulders. I jumped up, trying to pull myself together and at the same time duck the flames and stamp them out. I brushed the singeing ashes away from my face as I frantically grabbed for the door to open it.

"Help!" I shouted. "Help!" The door wouldn't open. Someone was holding it—someone strong, perhaps more than one person. I was trapped.

"Did you think we were gonna let niggers use our toilets? We'll burn you alive, girl," a voice shouted through the door. "There won't be enough of you left to worry about."

Source: Melba Pattillo Beals, *Warriors Don't Cry* (New York: Washington Square Press, 1994), pp. 55-56, 95-96, 115-16, 71, 136, 139-40, 148, 161, 163-64.

For the nine black students, the year that they spent at Central High was frightening and painful. Beals began writing her memoirs when she was eighteen. But she could not complete it until 1994 because she "could not face the ghosts that its pages called up." Eight of the students eventually left Little Rock. Elizabeth Eckford, perhaps the most traumatized of the group, remained in the city. In 1996, Heather Jurgensen, a sixteen year old student at a rural high school in Kansas decided to do her National History Day project on the "Little Rock Nine." Jurgensen was surprised to find Eckford still living in Little Rock. Eckford agreed to be interviewed by the high school student. In her interview, Eckford remembered a white student—Ken Reinhardt, Jr.—who back in 1957 always said "hello" to her and treated her like "any other student." For this, he was roughed up and received threatening phone calls.

Two of Jurgensen's classmates decided to do their History Day project on Reinhardt and other whites who supported civil rights activists. They tracked Reinhardt down in Louisville. Reinhardt, now a banker, not only agreed to be interviewed but flew to Little Rock to see

Eckford. The two had not seen each other since the 1957-58 school year. In a reunion made possible by three teenagers from an all-white rural high school, the two former classmates recalled Eckford's extraordinary courage and Reinhardt's simple acts of kindness that brought them together briefly in a crucial era of our nation's history.

A Segregationist Call to Arms

Some southern whites expressed their willingness to fight integration with violence. This sign was placed in the yards of people who supported the desegregation of Florida's schools during the 1959-60 school year:

DEATH TO ALL RACE MIXERS!
Keep White Public Schools
WHITE
BY
Massive Armed Force!
BE A
Paul Revere!
Rally Your Neighbors to
ARMS — SHOOT
The Race-Mixing
INVADERS!

Source: Langston Hughes, Milton Meltzer and C. Eric Lincoln, *A Pictorial History of Blackamericans* (New York: Crown Publishers, 1983), p. 312.

In Jail

Most civil rights activists had never been in jail before they began demonstrating. In his book, The

Children, David Halberstam describes the experience of one such activist:

Curtis Murphy had been one of the eighty-one demonstrators arrested [at the Nashville sit-in]. Somehow at the police station he had been quickly separated from the other students. It was Murphy's first venture into the black prison world, and it frightened him even more than being arrested. He had been placed in a holding pen with other prisoners, all black, and these were not pleasant young college students from middle-class homes: these were hard-core criminals. There he was in his best clothes—jacket and tie and a handsome topcoat; he knew he was out of place. He was soft and they were tough.

There was a man in particular who scared him, a huge, mean-looking man with very dark skin, perhaps six feet two and 230 pounds, with a great scar on his neck where he had been cut in some violent knife fight, most likely one of many. He had appraised Curtis carefully when he had arrived in jail, and given him a look which seemed to say, Boy, you are candy for the rest of us....

Curtis Murphy did not know very much about jail, but he knew instantly that nothing was going to happen this man did not sanction...Curtis rolled up his coat and tried to make it into a pillow and tried to read. As soon as he did, someone yelled for him to turn off the light, and he was scared by the voice...Just then he heard an even tougher voice, the voice of the black man with the cut on his throat. "Hey, schoolboy," the voice said....

"Yes," he answered, aware of how shaky and tentative his voice sounded.

"Schoolboy," the tough black man said...."I know why you're in here, schoolboy, and what you're doing, and you can keep the light on all you want, my young friend."

Source: David Halberstam, *The Children* (New York: Random House, 1998), pp. 149-50.

The Student Non-Violent Coordinating Committee's Statement of Purpose

At the conference that gave birth to the Student Non-Violent Coordinating Committee (SNCC), Marion Barry (the future mayor of Washington, D. C.) was elected the organization's first chairman. The SNCC asked Reverend James Lawson, who conducted classes on nonviolent civil disobedience for sit-in demonstrators, to draft its April 1960 "Statement of Purpose":

We affirm the philosophical or religious ideal of nonviolence as the foundation of our purpose, the presupposition of our faith, and the manner of our action. Nonviolence as it grows from Judaic-Christian tradition seeks a social order of justice permeated by love. Integration of human endeavor represents the crucial first step toward such a society.

Through nonviolence, courage displaces fear; love transforms hate. Acceptance dissipates prejudice; hope ends despair. Peace dominates war; faith reconciles doubt. Mutual regard cancels enmity. Justice for all overthrows injustice. The redemptive community supersedes systems of gross social immorality.

Love is the central motif of nonviolence. Love is the force by which God binds man to Himself and man to man. Such love goes to the extreme; it remains loving and forgiving even in the midst of hostility. It matches the capacity of evil to inflict suffering with an even more enduring capacity to absorb evil, all the while persisting in love.

By appealing to conscience and standing on the moral nature of human existence, nonviolence nurtures the atmosphere in which reconciliation and justice become actual possibilities.

Source: Peter Levy, ed., *Let Freedom Ring: A Documentary History of the Modern Civil Rights Movement* (New York: Praeger, 1992), pp. 74-75.

Freedom Rides

In 1946, the United States Supreme Court prohibited the segregation of interstate buses and trains. The following year, an interracial group of sixteen civil rights activists traveled through the South on a "Journey of Reconciliation" to test compliance with the court order. A number of the activists belonged to the Congress of Racial Equality (CORE), an interracial organization founded in 1942 to promote racial equality and harmony. In 1961, the Supreme Court expanded the ban on segregation to bus and train terminals. CORE decided to test this new ruling. White volunteers would ride in the back of interstate buses and blacks in the front. At every rest stop, blacks would go into "whites-only" waiting rooms and whites into "colored" waiting rooms. CORE felt that by such actions "we could count on the racists of the South to create a crisis so that the federal government would be compelled to enforce the law."

The "Freedom Rides" began on May 4, 1961 from Washington, D. C. The seven black and six white volunteers hoped to ride through the South and arrive in New Orleans on May 17, the anniversary date of the Brown *decision. The Freedom Ride proceeded without incident through the upper South. But violence engulfed the freedom riders in the Deep South. As CORE executive director James Farmer recalled, an angry mob awaited them in Anniston, Alabama:*

> When the Greyhound bus arrived in Anniston, there was a mob of white men standing there at the bus terminal. The members of the mob had their weapons—pistols, guns, blackjacks, clubs, chains,

knives—all in plain evidence. The Freedom Riders made a decision on the spot that discretion was the better part of valor in this case, and that they were not going to test the terminal facilities at Anniston. To do so would have been suicide. They told that decision to the driver, who prepared to drive the bus on. Before the bus pulled out, however, members of the mob took their sharp instruments and slashed tires. The bus got to the outskirts of Anniston and the tires blew out and the bus ground to a halt. Members of the mob had boarded cars and followed the bus, and now with the disabled bus standing there, the members of the mob surrounded it, held the door closed, and a member of the mob threw a firebomb into the bus, breaking a window to do so. Incidentally, there were some local policemen mingling with the mob, fraternizing with them while this was going on.

Source: Henry Hampton and Steve Fayer, eds., *Voices of Freedom: An Oral History of the Civil Rights Movement from the 1950s through the 1980s* (London: Vintage, 1995) p. 79.

Someone in the crowd yelled, "Let's roast the niggers!" With this, the mob tried to seal the Freedom Riders inside the burning bus. They were saved by the explosion of the bus' gas tank, which temporarily scattered the mob. When the mob moved back towards the bus, an Alabama state trooper stepped forward, identified himself and ordered the mob to disperse. Floyd Mann, the state's director of public

safety, sent the undercover trooper to protect the Freedom
Riders. Mann was not an integrationist. But he felt that it
was his duty to ensure their safety.

Blacks and Whites joined together to work for civil rights.

CORE *decided to call off the Freedom Ride because of*
the violence and because the bus company refused to risk
losing any more of its vehicles. But a group of students who
had led the sit-ins in Nashville decided to reassemble in
Birmingham and continue the Freedom Ride from there.
Diane Nash, leader of the Nashville group, recalled that
"[i]f the Freedom Riders had been stopped as a result of
violence, I strongly felt that the future of the movement was
going to be cut short. The impression would have been that
whenever a movement starts, all [you have to do] is attack it
with massive violence and the blacks [will] stop." The group
urged Nash to coordinate the Freedom Ride rather than
take part in it. She reluctantly agreed. This turned out to be
a wise decision. In Birmingham, police commissioner "Bull"
Connor arrested the new Freedom Riders and placed them

under "protective custody." When Connor dumped the Freedom Riders near the Alabama-Tennessee border at 2:00 A.M. the next morning, Nash was able to rescue them before the Ku Klux Klan could get at them.

The Kennedy administration was reluctant to intervene but it could not ignore the United States Supreme Court's order to integrate interstate transportation. The administration demanded protection for the Freedom Riders who were exercising their constitutional rights. Public safety director Mann assured federal officials that the state police would protect Freedom Riders on the highway between Birmingham and Montgomery. They would be protected by local police when they reached the city limits. Neither Mann nor the Freedom Riders knew that Montgomery police had conspired with the Ku Klux Klan to give them a fifteen-minute "grace period" to assault the Riders before they would move in.

John Lewis, who would later become chairman of SNCC and a Congressman from Georgia, was among the Freedom Riders arriving in Montgomery:

> ...when we arrived at the [Montgomery] bus station, it was eerie....It was so quiet, so peaceful, nothing. And the moment we started down the steps of that bus, there was an angry mob. People came out of nowhere—men, women, children, with baseball bats, clubs, chains—and there was no police official

around. They just started beating people. We tried to get all the women on the ride into a taxicab. There was one cab there, and this driver said he couldn't take the group because it was interracial....Then the mob turned on members of the press....[T]hey beat up all the reporters, then they turned on the black male members and white male members of the group....I think I was hit with a sort of crate thing that holds soda bottles—and left lying unconscious there, in the streets of Montgomery.

Source: Hampton and Fayer, pp. 86-87.

Fred Leonard, a black college freshman, was also on the bus. He remembered how the mob turned on Jim Zwerg when he stepped off the bus:

Everybody was feeling comfortable going into the terminal in Montgomery. We didn't see anybody, but we didn't see any police either. And then, all of a sudden, just like magic: white people, sticks, and bricks. "Nigger! Kill the niggers!"...Jim Zwerg was a white fellow from Madison, Wisconsin—he had a lot of nerve. I think that's what saved me, Bernard Lafayette, and Allen Cason, 'cause Jim Zwerg walked off the bus in front of us and it was like those people in the mob were possessed. They couldn't believe that there was a white man who would help us, and they

> grabbed him and pulled him into the mob. When we
> came off the bus, their attention was on him. It's like
> they didn't see the rest of us for about thirty seconds.
>
> Source: Hampton and Fayer, pp. 87-88.

*Leonard managed to escape the mob, but others
did not:*

> Later we heard the news about Jim Zwerg, about
> John Lewis, about William Barbee. William Barbee
> was damaged for life, really, Jim Zwerg for life. It's
> amazing that they're still living; they could have been
> killed. I think what saved them was this white fellow
> who was in the crowd shot a gun in the air, and if it
> was not for him, they would be dead.
>
> Source: Hampton and Fayer, p. 88.

*That "white fellow" was Floyd Mann. Mann witnessed
the events unfolding at the Montgomery bus station and
took action:*

> When the bus arrived at the Montgomery bus
> station, only the assistant director of public safety,
> Mr. W. R. Jones, and myself were there. Just as soon
> as the riders began to get off the bus I noticed these
> strange people all around the bus. I knew immediately
> they were Klansmen. No sooner had the Freedom

Riders gotten off the bus than a riot evolved...And there were no police around the bus station. We immediately sent for...state troopers. But before they could arrive, cars were set on fire, people were attacked. Newspaper people were beaten, cameras

Birmingham policeman holds a Black man while he orders his dog to attack. (AP/Wide World Photos)

busted. Those Freedom Riders, some of them were being beaten with baseball bats. Therefore, we had to threaten to take some lives ourselves unless the violence stopped immediately. So I just put my pistol to the head of one or two of those folks that was using baseball bats and told them unless they stopped immediately, they was going to be hurt. And it did stop the beaters.

Source: Hampton and Fayer, pp. 88-89.

All About CORE

In 1963, CORE put out a brochure entitled "All About CORE," explaining who they were and what they did:

...CORE sees discrimination as a problem for all Americans. Not just Negroes suffer from it and not just Negroes will profit when it is eliminated. Furthermore, Negroes alone cannot eliminate it. Equality cannot be seized any more than it can be given. It must be a shared experience.

CORE is an inter-racial group. Membership involves no religious affiliation. It is open to anybody who opposes racial discrimination, who wants to fight it and who will adhere to CORE's rules. The only people not welcome to CORE are "those Americans whose loyalty is primarily to a foreign power and those whose tactics and beliefs are contrary to democracy and human values." CORE has only one enemy: discrimination, and only one function: to fight that enemy. It has no desire to complicate its task by acquiring a subversive taint, and it avoids partisan politics of any kind....

A great deal has been achieved for civil rights through the courts, and legal action has an important place in the civil rights movement. But legal action is necessarily limited to lawyers. CORE's techniques enable large numbers of ordinary people to participate in campaigns to end discrimination.

Direct action has a value that goes beyond its visible accomplishments. To those who are the target of discrimination, it provides an alternative to bitterness or resignation and, to others, an alternative to mere expressions of sentiment....

Source: Levy, pp. 82-83.

Martin Luther King, Jr. Emerges as a Leader

Twenty-six year old Martin Luther King, Jr. had arrived in Montgomery to preach at the Dexter Avenue Baptist Church. He was nevertheless elected president of the Montgomery Improvement Association, which was to organize the bus boycott. On the evening of the boycott,

King had about twenty minutes to prepare his speech to inspire the city's black citizens to continue it:

There comes a time that people get tired. We are here this evening to say to those who have mistreated us so long that we are tired—tired of being segregated and humiliated; tired of being kicked about by the brutal feet of oppression.... For many years we have shown amazing patience. We have sometimes given our white brothers the feeling that we like the way we were being treated. But we come here tonight to be saved from that patience that makes us patient with anything less than freedom and justice. One of the glories of democracy is the right to protest for right... if you will protest courageously and yet with dignity and Christian love, when the history books are written in future generations the historians will pause and say, 'There lived a great people—a black people—who injected new meaning and dignity into the veins of civilization.' That is our challenge and our overwhelming responsibility.

Source: Williams, p. 76.

Letter from Birmingham Jail

Many groups criticized Martin Luther King, Jr. during the Birmingham campaign. The one group he felt compelled to answer was the white liberal clergymen who criticized

King for his impatience and his disregard for the city's laws.
He wrote the original draft of this letter in the margins of
newspapers smuggled in to him in a Birmingham jail:

...I am in Birmingham because injustice is here...

...I cannot sit idly by in Atlanta and not be concerned about what happens in Birmingham. Injustice anywhere is a threat to justice everywhere. We are caught in an inescapable network of mutuality tied in a single garment of destiny. Whatever affects one directly affects all indirectly. Never again can we afford to live with the narrow, provincial "outside agitator" idea. Anyone who lives inside the United States can never be considered an outsider anywhere in this country....

...We know through painful experience that freedom is never voluntarily given by the oppressor; it must be demanded by the oppressed. Frankly I have yet to engage in a direct action movement that was "well timed," according to the timetable of those who have not suffered unduly from the disease of segregation. For years now I have heard the word "Wait!" It rings in the ear of every Negro with piercing familiarity. This "wait" has almost always meant "never." We must come to see with the distinguished jurist of yesterday that "justice too long delayed is justice denied." We have waited for more than three hundred and forty years for our constitutional and God-given rights....

I guess it is easy for those who have never felt the stinging darts of segregation to say wait. But when you have seen vicious mobs lynch your mothers and fathers at will and drown your sisters and brothers at whim; when you have seen hate filled policemen curse, kick, brutalize, and even kill your black brothers and sisters with impunity; when you see the vast majority of your twenty million Negro brothers smothering in an air-tight cage of poverty in the midst of an affluent society; when you suddenly find your tongue twisted and your speech stammering as you seek to explain to your six year old daughter why she can't go to the public amusement park that has just been advertised on television, and see tears welling up in her little eyes when she is told that Funtown is closed to colored children, and see the depressing clouds of inferiority beginning to form in her little mental sky, and see her beginning to distort her little personality by unconsciously developing a bitterness toward white people; when you have to concoct an answer for a five year old son who is asking: "Daddy, why do white people treat colored people so mean?"; when you take a cross country drive and find it necessary to sleep night after night in the uncomfortable corners of your automobile because no motel will accept you; when you are humiliated day in and day out by nagging signs reading "white" men and "colored"; when your first name becomes "nigger" and your middle name becomes "boy" (however old you are) and your last name becomes "John," and when your wife and mother are never given the respected title "Mrs."; when you are harried by day and haunted by night by the fact that you are a Negro, living constantly at tip-toe stance never quite knowing what to expect next, and plagued with inner fears and outer resentments; when you are forever fighting a degenerating sense of "nobodiness";—then you will understand why we find it difficult to wait....

You express a great deal of anxiety over our willingness to break laws. This is certainly a legitimate concern. Since we so diligently urge people to obey the Supreme Court's decision of 1954 outlawing segregation in the public schools, it is rather strange and paradoxical to find us consciously breaking laws. One may well ask: "How can you advocate breaking some laws and obeying others?" The answer is found in the fact that there are two types of laws: There are *just* laws and there are *unjust* laws. I would be the first to advocate obeying just laws. One has not only a legal but a moral responsibility to obey just laws. Conversely, one has a moral responsibility to disobey unjust laws. I would agree with St. Augustine that "An unjust law is no law at all."...

...We can never forget that everything Hitler did in Germany was "legal" and everything the Hungarian freedom fighters did in Hungary was "illegal." It was "illegal" to aid and comfort a Jew in Hitler's Germany. But I am sure that, if I had lived in Germany during that time, I would have aided and comforted my Jewish brothers even though it was illegal. If I lived in a Communist country today where certain principles dear to the Christian faith are suppressed, I believe I would openly advocate disobeying these anti-religious laws....

Source: Martin Luther King, Jr., *Letter from Birmingham City Jail* (Philadelphia: American Friends Service Committee, 1963), *reprinted in* Herbert Aptheker, ed., *A Documentary History of the Negro People in the United States,* Vol. 7 (New York: Citadel, 1994), pp. 220-26.

✳ ✳ ✳

"I Have a Dream"

In 1941, union leader A. Philip Randolph had conceived a march on Washington, D. C. to protest discriminatory working conditions for African Americans. He was persuaded by President Franklin D. Roosevelt to postpone the march. When Randolph suggested such a march to commemorate the centennial of the Emancipation Proclamation, he received positive responses from numerous civil rights organizations. Randolph's assistant, Bayard

Rustin, tended to the thousands of details. On August 28, 1963, over 200,000 took part in the march that culminated in a rally in front of the Lincoln Memorial. For the sake of unity, march organizers persuaded SNCC chairman John Lewis to tone down parts of his speech that criticized the Kennedy administration, which had initially opposed the march. Martin Luther King, Jr. delivered the speech for which the march is best remembered. His speech was an eloquent plea for equality, integration and racial justice, excerpts from which follow:

...Five score years ago, a great American, in whose symbolic shadow we stand, signed the Emancipation Proclamation. This momentous decree came as the great beacon light of hope to millions of Negro slaves who had been seared in the flames of withering injustice. It came as the joyous daybreak to end the long night of their captivity.

But one hundred years later the Negro is still not free. One hundred years later, the life of the Negro is still sadly crippled by the manacles of segregation and the chains of discrimination. One hundred years later, the Negro lives on a lonely island of poverty in the midst of a vast ocean of material prosperity.... So we have come here today to dramatize the shameful condition.

In a sense we've come to our Nation's Capital to cash a check. When the architects of our republic wrote the magnificent words of the Constitution and the Declaration of Independence, they were signing a promissory note to which every American was to fall heir. This note was a promise that all men, yes, black men as well as white men, would be guaranteed the unalienable rights of life, liberty, and the pursuit of happiness.

It is obvious today that America has defaulted on this promissory note insofar as her citizens of color are concerned. Instead of honoring this sacred obligation, America has given the Negro people a bad check; a check which has come back marked "Insufficient Funds." We refuse to believe that the bank of justice is bankrupt. We refuse to believe that there are insufficient funds in the great vaults of opportunity of this nation....

...Now is the time to rise from the dark and desolate valley of segregation to the sunlit path of racial justice. Now is the time to open the doors of opportunity to all of God's children. Now is the time to lift our nation from the quicksands of racial injustice to the solid rock of brotherhood....

...There are those who are asking the devotees of civil rights, "When will you be satisfied?" We can never be satisfied as long our bodies, heavy with the fatigue of travel, cannot gain lodging in the motels of the highways and the hotels of the cities. We cannot be satisfied as long as the Negro's basic mobility is from a smaller ghetto to a larger one. We can never be satisfied as long as our children are stripped of their selfhood and robbed of their dignity by signs stating: "For Whites Only." We cannot be satisfied as long as a Negro in Mississippi cannot vote and a Negro in New York believes he has nothing for which to vote. No, no, we are not satisfied and we will not be satisfied until justice rolls down like the waters and righteousness like a mighty stream....

I say to you today, my friends, even though we face the difficulties and frustrations of the moment I still have a dream. It is a dream deeply rooted in the American dream. I have a dream that one day this nation will rise up and live out the true meaning of its creed: "We hold these truths to be self-evident that all men are created equal."

I have a dream that one day on the red hills of Georgia the sons of former slaves and the sons of former slaveowners will be able to sit down together at the table of brotherhood.

I have a dream that one day even the State of Mississippi, a state sweltering with the heat of injustice, sweltering with the heat of oppression, will be transformed into an oasis of freedom and justice. I have a dream that my four little children will one day live in a nation where they will not be judged by the color of their skin but by the content of their character. I have a dream today.

I have a dream that one day down in Alabama with its vicious racists, with its Governor having his lips dripping with the words of interposition and nullification—one day right there in Alabama, little black boys and black girls will be able to join hands with little white boys and white girls as sisters and brothers.

I have a dream today....

This is our hope. This is the faith that I go back to the South with....With this faith we will be able to work together, to pray together, to struggle together, to go to jail together, to stand up for freedom together, knowing that we will be free one day....

...From every mountainside, let freedom ring. And when we allow freedom to ring, when we let it ring from every village, from every hamlet, from every state and every city, we will be able to speed up that day when all of God's children, black men and white men, Jews and Gentiles, Protestants and Catholics, will be able to join hands and sing in the words of the old Negro spiritual: "Free at last! free at last! thank God almighty, we are free at last!"

Source: Aptheker, pp. 250-54.

Kennedy, Johnson, and The Civil Rights Act of 1964

During the waning years of the Reconstruction Era, Radical Republicans managed to enact the Civil Rights Act of 1875. It forbade racial discrimination in public transportation, accommodations (hotels), and restaurants. Few states, however, vigorously enforced the act. In 1883, the United States Supreme Court ruled that the act was unconstitutional. It would take almost a hundred years for Congress to enact another such measure—the Civil Rights Act of 1964.

President John F. Kennedy received overwhelming support from African Americans in the 1960 election. But due to his narrow victory and his reliance on southern Democrats in Congress, Kennedy was reluctant to move on civil rights. He focused instead on foreign affairs. His coolness towards civil rights was shaken by events in the South, especially the brutal treatment of black youths in Birmingham. On June 11, 1963, Kennedy proposed a civil rights bill and made a bold televised speech in support of civil rights, an excerpt from which follows:

We preach freedom around the world, and we mean it, and we cherish our freedom here at home, but are we to say to the world, and much more importantly, to each other that this is the land of the free except for the Negroes; that we have no second class citizens except Negroes; that we have no class or caste system, no ghettoes, no master race except with respect to Negroes?

Now the time has come for this Nation to fulfill its promise. The events in Birmingham and elsewhere have so increased the cries for equality that no city or State or legislative body can prudently choose to ignore them.

The fires of frustration and discord are burning in every city, North and South, where legal remedies are not at hand. Redress is sought in the streets, in demonstrations, parades, and protests which create tensions and threaten violence and threaten lives.

We face, therefore, a moral crisis as a country and as a people. It cannot be met by repressive police action. It cannot be left to increased demonstrations in the streets. It cannot be quieted by token moves or talk. It is time to act in the Congress, in your State and local legislative body and, above all, in all of our daily lives....

I am, therefore, asking Congress to enact legislation giving all Americans the right to be served in facilities which are open to the public— hotels, restaurants, theaters, retail stores, and similar establishments.

This seems to me to be an elementary right. Its denial is an arbitrary indignity that no American in 1963 should have to endure, but many do.

Source: : Radio and Television Report to the American People on Civil Rights, June 11, 1963. U.S. President, *Public Papers of the Presidents of the United States* (Washington, D.C.: United States Government Printing Office, 1964), John F. Kennedy, 1963, pp. 468-71, *reprinted in* Thomas West and James Mooney, eds., *To Redeem a Nation: A History and Anthology of the Civil Rights Movement* (St. James, NY: Brandywine Press, 1993), pp. 164-65.

Kennedy's proposed civil rights bill had no chance of passage under his leadership. Unlike Kennedy, his successor, Lyndon B. Johnson, knew poverty and racism first hand. As president, he was determined to eliminate both. Using his political skills and the martyred image of Kennedy, Johnson was able to push the legislation through Congress. The Civil Rights Act of 1964 was the most significant law affecting African Americans since the Reconstruction Era. The Act made it illegal for privately owned restaurants, theaters and other "public accommodations" to segregate or turn away customers on the basis of race or color. It also prohibited private businesses from hiring and firing employees on the basis of race or color. Major features of the act are summarized below:

Title I: Prohibited the unequal application of voter registration requirements.

Title II: Outlawed discrimination by hotels, restaurants, theatres and other public accommodations.

> Title IV: Authorized the U.S. Attorney General to
> file suits to enforce the desegregation of
> public schools.
>
> Title VII: Barred discrimination by employers on
> the basis of race, color, religion, sex or
> national origin.

The Johnson administration adopted a policy requiring businesses, educational institutions and government agencies to be represented by a certain proportion of racial minorities and women. This "affirmative action" policy tried to ensure access for those previously denied jobs and education on account of race and gender.

George Wallace's Attack on the Civil Rights Act of 1964

Vowing never to be "out-niggered" again, George Wallace became the most visible advocate of segregation among southern politicians. His attacks on civil rights legislation, related Supreme Court rulings, communism and "left-wing" liberalism made him a hero among white conservatives. On July 4, 1964, Wallace attacked Congress and President Lyndon B. Johnson for enacting the Civil Rights Act of 1964:

> We come today in deference to the memory of
> those stalwart patriots who on July 4, 1776, pledged

their lives, their fortunes, and their sacred honor to establish and =defend the proposition that governments are created by the people, empowered by the people, derive their just powers from the consent of the people, and must forever remain subservient to the will of the people....

It is therefore a cruel irony that the President of the United States has only yesterday signed into law the most monstrous piece of legislation (Civil Rights Act of 1964) ever enacted by the United States Congress.

It is a fraud, a sham, and a hoax.

This bill will live in infamy. To sign it into law at any time is tragic. To do so upon the eve of the celebration of our independence insults the intelligence of the American people.

It dishonors the memory of countless thousands of our dead who offered up their very lives in defense of principles which this bill destroys.

Never before in the history of this nation have so many human and property rights been destroyed by a single enactment of the Congress. It is an act of tyranny. It is the assassin's knife stuck in the back of liberty.

With this assassin's knife and a blackjack in the hand of the Federal force-cult, the left-wing liberals will try to force us back into bondage. Bondage to a tyranny more brutal than that imposed by the British monarchy which claimed power to rule over the lives of our forefathers under sanction of the Divine Right of kings.

Today, this tyranny is imposed by the central government which claims the right to rule over our lives under sanction of the omnipotent black-robed despots who sit on the bench of the United States Supreme Court.

This bill is fraudulent in intent, in design, and in execution....

It threatens our freedom of speech, of assembly, ofassociation, and makes the exercise of these Freedoms a federal crime under certain conditions....

Ministers, lawyers, teachers, newspapers, and every private citizen must guard his speech and watch his actions to avoid the deliberately imposed booby traps put into this bill. It is designed to make Federal crimes of our customs, beliefs, and traditions....

I am having nothing to do with enforcing a law that will destroy our free enterprise system. I am having nothing to do with enforcing a law that will destroy neighborhood schools. I am having nothing to do with enforcing a law that will destroy the rights of private property....

Source: "Speech Prepared for Delivery by George C. Wallace," Southeastern Fairgrounds, Atlanta, Georgia, July 4, 1964, pp. 1-16, George Wallace Papers, McCain Library and Archives, University of Southern Mississippi.

Odyssey of Fanny Lou Hamer

Fanny Lou Hamer epitomized the SNCC's hopes for the Deep South. She was born and raised in rural Mississippi, the twentieth child born to a sharecropping family in Montgomery County. Her power to lead came from within, awakened by the civil rights movement. She was also not intimidated by powerful opponents.

Hamer had been unhappy with the South's political and economic system for some time when she attended a voter registration meeting in 1962:

> ...I been sick of this system as long as I can remember...I have worked as hard as anybody. I have been picking cotton and would be so hungry and... wondering what I was gone cook that night, but you see, all of them things were wrong[.]
>
> Source: Fannie Lou Hamer, mass meeting, Hattiesburg, Mississippi, 1963, Moses Moon Collection, Program in African American Culture, Archives, National Museum of American History, Smithsonian Institution, Washington, D.C., *reprinted in* Vicki Crawford, Jacqueline Anne Rouse and Barbara Woods, eds., *Women in the Civil Rights Movement: Trailblazers & Torchbearers, 1941-1965* (Bloomington: Indiana University Press, 1990), p. 211.

Hamer saw voting rights as a crucial first step in dismantling the oppressive system. She therefore volunteered to register to vote. When she returned from the courthouse, Hamer saw how swiftly the white establishment clamped down on efforts by black sharecroppers to gain political power:

...Reverend Jeff Sunny drove me out to the rural area where I had been working as a timekeeper and sharecropper for eighteen years. When I got there I was already fired. My children met and told me, "Mama, this man is hot! Said you will have to go back and withdraw [your registration application] or you will have to leave." ...It wasn't too long before my husband came and he said the same thing. I walked in the house, set down on the side of my little daughter's bed, and then this white man walked over and said, "Pap, did you tell Fannie Lou what I said?" I said, "He did." "Well, Fannie Lou, you will have to go down and withdraw or you will have to leave." And I addressed and told him, as we have always had to say "Mr., I didn't register for you; I was trying to register for myself." He said, "We're not ready for that in Mississippi." He wasn't ready, but I been ready a long time. I had to leave that same night.

Source: Crawford, Rouse and Woods, p. 209.

Not only did Hamer refuse to withdraw her application, she became a voter registration recruiter. For her actions, Hamer was shot at and arrested and in jail, she was brutally beaten.

Hamer became a key organizer of "Freedom Summer" 1964. She also helped to found the Mississippi Freedom Democratic Party (MFDP) that year. As Hamer explained

in a 1967 interview, civil rights activists formed MFDP
because blacks continued to be excluded from the state's
electoral politics:

> We have to build our own power. We have to win
> every single political office we can, where we have a
> majority of black people....The question for black
> people is not, when is the white man going to give
> us our rights, or when is he going to give us good
> education for our children, or when is he going to
> give us jobs—if the white man gives you anything—
> just remember when he get ready he will take it right
> back. We have to take [power] for ourselves.
>
> Source: Aptheker, p. 465.

The MFDP held elections (open to all races) for
delegates to the 1964 Democratic National Convention
in Atlantic City, New Jersey. At the Convention, MFDP
delegates challenged the seating of Mississippi's all-white
delegation before the Democratic Party's Credentials
Committee. President Lyndon Johnson had the nomination
locked up but feared losing southern white support in the
general election. Johnson pressured liberal politicians such
as Hubert Humphrey and black leaders such as Martin
Luther King, Jr. to quiet the demands of the MFDP.
Humphrey, aspiring to be Johnson's running mate, had his
protege, Walter Mondale, work out a compromise giving
the MFDP two "at-large" seats along with a promise to ban

racial discrimination at the 1968 convention. MFDP
delegates voted to reject the compromise. Hamer was
MFDP's star witness before the Credentials Committee.
She made an impassioned plea:

> If the Freedom Democratic Party is not seated
> now, I question America. Is this America? The land of
> the free and the home of the brave? Where we have to
> sleep with our telephones off the hook, because our
> lives be threatened daily?...They beat me...with the
> long, flat blackjack. I screamed to God in pain.
>
> Source: Williams, pp. 241-42.

Hamer then broke down and cried before television
cameras providing live national coverage of the testimony.
Rita Schwerner, widow of the CORE worker murdered in
Mississippi, sat next to Hamer, waiting to testify. Johnson
saw the televised proceedings and was furious. He ordered
aides to phone the television networks to announce a
presidential press conference immediately. Although they did
not see the ending of Hamer's testimony, people across the
nation were moved by the courage and commitment of this
woman from rural Mississippi.

Bob Moses and the Voter Registration Campaign

Bob Moses saw voting as the most effective means
of empowering African Americans. He therefore led a

campaign to register black voters in rural Mississippi. The work was difficult and dangerous. Most rural blacks were employed by white planters and many lived on the planters' property. They therefore were hesitant to take any action that would antagonize their bosses and landlords. Voter registration workers faced violence and intimidation from white citizens who did not wish to share political power with African Americans. In an interview, Moses described voter registration process and the accompanying dangers:

...[W]e went around house-to-house, door-to-door in the hot sun everyday because the most important thing was to convince the local townspeople that...we were people who were responsible. What do you tell somebody when you go to their door? Well, first you tell them who you are, what you're trying to do, that you're working on voter registration. You have a form that you try to get them to fill out....

Now we did this for about two weeks and finally began to get results. That is, people began to go down to Magnolia, Mississippi, which is the county seat of Pike County and attempt to register. In the meantime...people from Amite and Walthall County, which are the two adjacent countries to Pike County, came over asking us if we wouldn't accompany them in schools in their counties so they could go down and try to register also. And this point should be made quite clear, because many people have been critical of going into such tough counties so early in the game.... The problem is that you can't be in a position of turning down the tough areas because the people then, I think, would simply lose confidence in you; so, we accepted this.

We planned to make another registration attempt on the 19th of August....This was the day that Curtis Dawson, Preacher Knox and I were to go down and try to register....[We] were accosted by Billy Jack Caston and some other boys. I was severely beaten. I remember very sharply that I didn't want to go immediately back into McComb because my shirt was very bloody and I figured that if we went back in we would probably be fighting everybody. So, instead, we went back out to Steptoe's where we washed down before we came back into McComb....

We felt it was extremely important that we try and go back to town immediately so the people in that county wouldn't feel that we had been frightened off by the beating and before they could get a chance there to rally their forces.

Source: Clayborne Carson et al, *Eyes on the Prize Civil Rights Reader* (New York: Penguin Books, 1987), pp. 170-73.

J. Edgar Hoover and Martin Luther King, Jr.

The Civil Rights Movement relied heavily on the federal government to protect their activists from racist organizations and local officials. This was limited by the reluctance of federal officials, from the president down, to interfere in state and local jurisdictions. It was further circumvented by the beliefs and attitude of the director of the Federal Bureau of Investigation (FBI), J. Edgar Hoover. The director was a racist who believed that "Negroes' brains are twenty percent smaller than white peoples'." (Taylor Branch, Pillar of Fire: America in the King Years, 1963-65 *(New York: Touchstone Books, 1988), p. 536.)* *Hoover also accused civil rights organizations of being controlled by communists. He launched a personal vendetta against Martin Luther King, Jr. after King won the Nobel Peace Prize. Hoover called King "the most notorious liar in the country." He tried to get other civil rights organizations, such as the NAACP, to denounce King and the SCLC. FBI wiretaps on King revealed that he was engaging in extramarital affairs. In November of 1964, Hoover sent King a "suicide package" containing recordings of his sexual activities along with a contrived anonymous letter denouncing King as "a great liability for all of us Negroes." The letter told King that "your end is approaching." "You are done," it stated, "There is but one way out for you. You better take it before your filthy, abnormal fraudulent self is bared to the nation."* (Branch, p. 528.)

Debates Over a Multiracial Civil Rights Movement

Disagreements emerged early in the SNCC over its composition and direction. Early SNCC leaders, such as John Lewis and Bob Moses, advocated an integrated organization. Later SNCC leaders, such as Stokely Carmichael, believed it should be an exclusively black organization.

In November of 1963, SNCC members gathered in Greenville, Mississippi to decide whether to bring large numbers of white college students into the 1964 Mississippi Summer Projects voter registration drive. In his article, "Forgotten Greenville: SNCC and the Lessons of 1963," Nicolaus Mills states that "Greenville was one of the last times in the 1960s when blacks and whites in SNCC thought of themselves as a 'band of brothers' yet still questioned the value of an integrated civil rights movement." He notes that "to look back at Greenville is to see how even in the best of times building a multiracial civil rights movement troubled its most committed participants and, in particular if they were black, made them vulnerable to the charge that they were substituting a white agenda for authentic racial change."

Donna Moses opposed the inclusion of white students because she feared that it would arouse Mississippi's white community. She also noted that what support the students might provide would disappear after August, when the fall semester began. Charlie Cobb worried about the role that whites would play in the Project. Cobb did not believe that whites intended take over the Project but he feared that they would "gravitate to positions of authority." "The tendency," according to Cobb, "is for the whites to articulate the demands of Negroes and the Negro person while the Negro kids stand quietly on the side. This is not done on purpose by whites, but it is done." Mendy Samstein echoed Cobb's concern. "If thousands of whites come down," Samstein felt that there would be "the problem of relationships between black, and whites. Whites convincing blacks of their rights—this entrenches the concept of white supremacy." Ivanhoe Donaldson wondered how an SNCC that depended on whites to carry out its Summer Project would appeal to young blacks. Donaldson noted that it might be an emotional reaction but he felt strongly about a black-led movement.

John Lewis supported the inclusion of white students because he felt that Mississippi blacks were "invisible to white people." He felt that the only way for the nation to see their plight was for hundreds of whites to join in the Mississippi Summer Project. Bob Moses felt that if SNCC excluded whites it "was in danger of leading a 'racist movement' in which color, not moral conduct, separated friend friend from foe." In his view, "[t]he only way you can break this down is to have white people working alongside you. Then it changes the whole complexion of what you're doing so it isn't any longer a Negro fighting white." Moses stated that "I'm not going to be part of an *organization that says, 'No white people are going to be head of a project because they're white....I'll gladly leave if that's the kind of organization you want to run."*

Fannie Lou Hamer agreed. "If we're trying to break down this barrier of segregation," she declared, "we can't segregate ourselves."

In the end, SNCC's executive committee decided to sanction the use of white student volunteers. It felt that without their presence, SNCC would be fighting an invisible and hopeless cause.

Later SNCC

At a May 1966 SNCC meeting, John Lewis resigned as chairman and James Forman resigned as executive secretary. Lewis was replaced by Stokely Carmichael. Under Carmichael's leadership, SNCC purged its white members and headed in a separatist direction. This position was outlined in the New York Times on August 5, 1966:

> In an attempt to find a solution to our dilemma, we propose that our organization (SNCC) should be black-staffed, black-controlled, and black-financed. We do not want to fall into a similar dilemma that other civil rights organizations have fallen. If we continue to rely upon white financial support we will find ourselves entwined in the tentacles of the white power complex that controls this country. It is also

important that a black organization (devoid of cultism) be projected to our people so that it can be demonstrated that such organizations are viable.

More and more we see black people in this country being used as a tool of the white liberal establishment. Liberal whites have not begun to address themselves to the real problem of black people in this country; witness their bewilderment, fear, and anxiety when nationalism is mentioned concerning black people. An analysis of their (white liberal) reaction to the word alone (nationalism) reveals a very meaningful attitude of whites of any ideological persuasion toward blacks in this country. It means previous solutions to black problems in this country have been made in the interests of those whites dealing with these problems and not in the best interests of black people in this country. Whites can only subvert our true search and struggle for self-determination, self-identification, and liberation in this country. Re-evaluation of the white and black roles must now take place so that whites no longer designate roles that black people play but rather black people define white people's roles....

...These facts do not mean that whites cannot help. They can participate on a voluntary basis. We can contract work out to them, but in no way can they participate on a policy-making level.

> The charge may be made that we are "racists," but whites who are sensitive to our problems will realize that we must determine our own destiny.
>
> Source: Aptheker, pp. 438-39.

Selma, Johnson and the Voting Rights Act of 1965

A handful of civil rights activists began a grassroots voter registration campaign in Selma, Alabama in 1961. They faced daily threats and intimidation from racist organizations and Selma's brutal police force. Selma became a focal point of the civil rights movement when Martin Luther King, Jr. came to organize voting rights demonstrations in the city. King and other civil rights leaders were trying to convince President Johnson to introduce a federal voting rights bill. Johnson, who had struggled to get the Civil Rights Act of 1964 through Congress, felt that the nation was not ready for further major civil rights legislation. King hoped to nudge Johnson with the demonstrations. On Sunday, March 7, 1965, civil rights demonstrators began a march from Selma to the state capital in Montgomery. At Pettus Bridge on the outskirts of Selma, the police, led by Sheriff Jim Clark, attacked the demonstrators. They shot tear gas into the ranks of the marchers, then attacked on horseback with clubs. SNCC chairman John Lewis, who was leading the march, suffered a fractured skull. News of the police attack on "Bloody

Sunday" brought hundreds of civil rights sympathizers to Selma. One of them, a northern white minister, was beaten to death in the streets of Selma. The national outrage over events in Selma compelled Johnson to introduce a voting rights bill. Johnson appealed to the nation's conscience as he introduced what would become the Voting Rights Act of 1965 to a joint session of Congress:

I speak tonight for the dignity of man and the destiny of democracy. I urge every member of both parties, Americans of all religions and of all colors, from every section of this country, to join me in that cause.

...Our mission is at once the oldest and the most basic of this country: to right wrong, to do justice, to serve man....Rarely in any time does an issue lay bare the secret heart of America itself. Rarely are we met with a challenge, not to our growth or abundance, or our welfare or our security, but rather to the values and the purposes and the meaning of our beloved nation.

The issue of equal rights for American Negroes is such an issue. And should we defeat every enemy and should we double our wealth and conquer the stars and still be unequal to this issue, then we will have failed as a people and as a nation. For with a country as with a person, "What is a man profited, if he shall gain the whole world, and lose his own soul?"

There is no Negro problem. There is no Southern problem. There is no Northern problem. There is only an American problem. And we are met here tonight as Americans, not as Democrats or Republicans, we are met here as Americans to solve the problem.

...As a man whose roots go deeply into Southern soil I know how agonizing racial feelings are. I know how difficult it is to reshape attitudes and the structure of our society. But a century has passed, more than a hundred years, since the Negro was freed. And he is not fully free tonight....

The time for justice has now come....And when it does, I think that the day will brighten the lives of every American. For Negroes are not the only victims. How many white children have gone uneducated, how many white families have lived in stark poverty, how many whites have been scarred by fear because we wasted our energy and substance to maintain the barriers of hatred and terror.

So I say to all of you here and to all in the nation tonight, that those who appeal to you to hold on to the past do so at the cost of denying you your future. This great, rich, restless country can offer opportunity and education and hope to all—all black and white, all North and South, sharecropper, and city dweller. These are the enemies—poverty, ignorance, disease. They are enemies, not our fellow men, not our neighbor, and these enemies too...we shall overcome....

Source: Lyndon B. Johnson, "Address Before a Joint Session of Congress," March 15, 1965, *reprinted in* Levy, pp. 159-62.

Coming of Age in Mississippi

Anne Moody was born and raised in rural Mississippi. As a child, she learned about Emitt Till's lynching. This made Moody realize her own vulnerability as an African American living in the Deep South. When Moody went off to college, she became active in the civil rights movement. Moody learned that her involvement had an impact on her family back home:

In mid-September I was back on campus. But didn't very much happen until February when the NAACP held its annual convention in Jackson. They were having a whole lot of interesting speakers: Jackie Robinson, Floyd Patterson, Curt Flood, Margaretta Belafonte, and many others....I was so excited that I sent one of the leaflets home to Mama and asked her to come.

Three days later I got a letter from Mama with dried-up tears on it, forbidding me to go to the convention. It went on for more than six pages. She said if I didn't stop [my activities] she would come to

Tougaloo and kill me herself. She told me about the time I last visited her, on Thanksgiving, and she had picked me up at the bus station. She said she picked me up because she was scared some white in my hometown would try to do something to me. She said the sheriff had been by, telling her I was messing around with that NAACP group. She said he told her if I didn't stop it, I could not come back there any more. He said they didn't need any of those NAACP people messing around in Centreville. She ended the letter by saying that she had burned the leaflet I sent her. "Please don't send any more of that stuff here. I don't want nothing to happen to us here," she said. "If you keep that up, you will never be able to come home again."

Source: Anne Moody, *Coming of Age in Mississippi* (New York: The Dial Press, 1968), p. 233.

Nation of Islam

The Nation of Islam was founded in 1930 by Wallace D. Fard. When Fard disappeared in 1934, Elijah Muhammad assumed leadership. "Black Muslims," as they came to be called, taught that blacks in America had been oppressed by the white race of devils for four hundred years. They insist, however, that blacks will be liberated by turning to Islam. The Nation of Islam compels its members to follow a strict regimen, including frequent daily prayer; no tobacco, alcohol or pork consumption; and adherence to a rigid code of moral behavior. In his Message to the Blackman in America *(1965), Elijah Muhammad outlined the goals and objectives of the Nation of Islam:*

What Do the Muslims Want?

This is the question asked most frequently by both the whites and the blacks. The answers to this question I shall state as simply as possible.

1. We want freedom. We want a full and complete freedom.

2. We want justice. Equal justice under the law. We want justice applied equally to all regardless of creed, class or color.

3. We want equality of opportunity. We want equal membership in society with the best in civilized society.

4. We want our people in America whose parents or grandparents were descendants from slaves to be allowed to establish a separate state or territory of their own—either on this continent or elsewhere. We believe that our former slave-masters are obligated to provide such land and that our area must be fertile and minerally rich. We believe that our former slave-masters are obligated to maintain and supply our needs in this separate territory for the next 20 or 25

years until we are able to produce and supply our own needs.

Since we cannot get along with them in peace and equality after giving them 400 years of our sweat and blood and receiving in return some of the worst treatment human beings have ever experienced, we believe our contributions to this land and the suffering forced upon us by white America justifies our demand for complete separation in a state or territory of our own.

5. We want freedom for all Believers of Islam now held in federal prisons. We want freedom for all black men and women now under death sentence in innumerable prisons in the North as well as the South.

We want every black man and woman to have the freedom to accept or reject being separated from the slave-masters' children and establish a land of their own.

We know that the above plan for the solution of the black and white conflict is the best and only answer to the problem between two people.

6. We want an immediate end to the police brutality and mob attacks against the so-called Negro throughout the United States.

We believe that the Federal government should intercede to see that black men and women tried in white courts receive justice in accordance with the laws of the land, or allow us to build a new nation for ourselves, dedicated to justice, freedom and liberty.

7. As long as we are not allowed to establish a state or territory of our own, we demand not only equal justice under the laws of the United States but equal employment opportunities—NOW!

We do not believe that after 400 years of free or nearly free labor, sweat and blood, which has helped America become rich and powerful, so many thousands of black people should have to subsist on relief or charity or live in poor houses.

8. We want the government of the United States to exempt our people from ALL taxation as long as we are deprived of equal justice under the laws of the land.

9. We want equal education—but separate schools up to 16 for boys and 18 for girls on the conditions that the girls be sent to women's colleges and universities. We want all black children educated, taught and trained by their own teacher.

Under such school system we believe we will make a better nation of people. The United States government should provide free all necessary text books and equipment, schools and college buildings. The Muslim teachers shall be left free to teach and train their people in the ways of righteousness, decency and self respect.

10. We believe that intermarriage or race mixing should be prohibited. We want the religion of Islam taught without hindrance or suppression.

Source: Elijah Muhammad, *Message to the Blackman in America* (Chicago: Muhammad Mosque of Islam No. 2, 1965), *reprinted in* West and Mooney, pp. 185-87.

Malcolm X on Economic Nationalism

Malcolm X tied economics to the nationalist aspirations of blacks in the United States and abroad:

...The economic philosophy of black nationalism only means that our people need to be re-educated into the importance of...controlling the economy of the community in which we live....[W]e have to learn how to own and operate the businesses of our community and develop them into some type of industry that will enable us to create employment for the people of our community so that they won't have to constantly be involved in picketing and boycotting other people in other communities in order to get a job.

Also...we have to learn the importance of spending our money in the community where we live. Anyone who knows the basic principles of economics must be aware of the fact that when you take the money out of the neighborhood in which you live and spend it in an integrated neighborhood...the neighborhood in which you spend your money becomes wealthier and wealthier, and the neighborhood out of which you take your money becomes poorer and poorer. And this is one of the reasons why wherever you find Negroes, a slum condition usually develops, or we have to live in the ghetto—because all our wealth is spent elsewhere....

Just as it took nationalism to bring about the independence of our brothers and sisters in Africa and Asia, the goal or the objective of the political, social, and economic philosophy of black nationalism is designed to bring about the complete independence of the black people in this country by making us become consciously involved in controlling our own community. Once we can control our own communities, then perhaps we will later be able to control our own country...and in some way have control over our own destiny....This philosophy in itself will bring about the independent thinking of the black people in this country, and eventually lead to the complete physical independence of the black people in this country.

Source: George Breitman, *The Last Year of Malcolm X: The Evolution of a Revolutionary* (New York: Schocken Books, 1968), pp. 88-89.

Malcolm X's Pilgrimage to Mecca

After departing from the Nation of Islam, Malcolm X made a pilgrimage to Mecca. It was an eye-opening experience for him, as described in a newspaper account of a letter by Malcolm X to a friend from Saudi Arabia, an excerpt from which follows:

There are Muslims of all colors and ranks here in Mecca from all parts of this earth.

During the past seven days of this holy pilgrimage...I have eaten from the same plate, drank from the same glass, slept on the same bed or rug, while praying to the same God...with fellow-Muslims whose skin was the whitest of white, whose eyes were the bluest of blue, and whose hair was the blondest of blond—yet it was the first time in my life that I didn't see them as "white" men. I could look into their faces and see that these didn't regard themselves as "white."

Their belief in the Oneness of God (Allah) had actually removed the "white" from their minds, which automatically changed their attitude and behavior toward people of colors. Their belief in the Oneness of God has actually made them so different from American whites, their outer physical characteristics played no part at all in my mind during all my close associations with them....I have never before witnessed such sincere hospitality and the practice of true brotherhood as I have seen and experienced during this pilgrimage here in Arabia.

Source: Malcolm X and Alex Haley, *The Autobiography of Malcolm X* (New York: Ballantine Books, 1999), pp. 346-47.

✳✳✳

Malcolm X on What "Well-Intentioned" Whites Can Do

Malcolm X was disillusioned by the revelation that Elijah Muhammad had been engaging in illicit affairs with his female assistants. His pilgrimage to Mecca convinced him to reject Elijah Muhammad's doctrines, particularly those labeling all whites as "devils." This, however, did not mean that Malcolm X now advocated integration. In his Autobiography, *he spelled out what well-intentioned whites could do to help resolve the race problem:*

I knew, better than most Negroes, how many white people truly wanted to see American racial problems solved. I knew that many whites were as frustrated as Negroes. I'll bet I got fifty letters some days from white people. The white people in meeting audiences would throng around me, asking me, after I had addressed them somewhere, "What can a sincere white person do?"

When I say that here now, it makes me think about that little co-ed I told you about, the one who flew from her New England college down to New York and came up to me in the Nation of Islam's restaurant in Harlem, and I told her that there was "nothing" she could do. I regret that I told her that. I wish that now I knew her name, or where I could telephone her, or write to her, and tell her what I tell white people now when they present themselves as being sincere, and ask me, one way or another, the same thing that she asked.

...I tell sincere white people, "Work in conjunction with us—each of us working among our own kind." Let sincere white individuals find all other white people they can who feel as they do—and let them form their own all-white groups, to work trying to convert other white people who are thinking and acting so racist. Let sincere whites go and teach non-violence to white people!

Source: Malcolm X, pp. 383-84.

Angry Children of Malcolm X

In an article entitled "The Angry Children of Malcolm X" (1966), Julius Lester discussed Malcolm X's legacy:

This is their message: The days of singing freedom songs and the days of combating bullets and billy clubs with love are over. "We Shall Overcome" sounds old, out-dated....The world of black Americans is different from that of the white American. This difference comes not only from the segregation imposed on the black, but it also comes from the way of life he has evolved for himself under these conditions. Yet, America has always been uneasy with this separate world in its midst. Feeling most comfortable when the black man emulates the ways and manners of white Americans, America has, at the same time, been stolidly unwilling to let the black man be assimilated into the mainstream.

With its goal of assimilation on the basis of equality, the civil rights movement was once the great hope of black men and liberal whites. In 1960 and 1961 Negroes felt that if only Americans knew the wrongs and sufferings they had to endure, these wrongs would be righted and all would be well.... and the Reverend Dr. Martin Luther King, Jr. was the knight going forth to prove to the father that he was worthy of becoming a member of the family. But there was something wrong with this attitude and young Negroes began to feel uneasy. Was this not another form of the bowing and scraping their grandparents had to do to get what they wanted? Were they not acting once again as the white man wanted and expected them to? And why should they have to be brutalized, physically and spiritually, for what every other American had at birth?...

More than any other person Malcolm X was responsible for the new militancy that entered The Movement in 1965. Malcolm X said aloud those things which Negroes had been saying among themselves....

Now the Negro is beginning to study his past, to learn those things that have been lost, to recreate what the white man destroyed in him and to destroy that which the white man put instead. He has stopped being a Negro and has become a black man in recognition of his new identity, his real identity. "Negro" is an American invention which shut him off from those of the same color in Africa. He recognizes now that part of himself is in Africa....

Many things that have happened in the past six years have had little or no meaning for most whites, but have had vital meaning for Negroes. Wasn't it only a month after the March on Washington that four children were killed in a church bombing in Birmingham? Whites could feel morally outraged, but they couldn't feel the futility, despair and anger that swept through The Nation within a nation—Black America. There were limits to how much one people could endure and Birmingham Sunday possibly marked that limit....

Now it is over. America has had chance after chance to show that it really meant "that all men are endowed with certain inalienable rights."...Now it is over. The days of singing freedom songs and the days of combating bullets and billy clubs with Love....As one SNCC veteran put it after the Mississippi March, "Man, the people are too busy getting ready to fight to bother with singing anymore." And as for Love? That's always been better done in bed than on the picket line and marches....They used to sing "I Love Everybody" as they ducked bricks and bottles. Now they sing:

Too much love,

Too much love,

Nothing kills a nigger like

Too much love....

Source: Julius Lester, *Sing Out* (October/November 1966), pp. 120-25, *reprinted in* Levy, pp. 177-80.

The Fire Next Time

In The Fire Next Time *(1963), the black novelist and essayist James Baldwin critiqued the views of white liberals on race and integration:*

White Americans find it as difficult as white people elsewhere do to divest themselves of the notion that they are in possession of some intrinsic value that black people need, or want. And this assumption—which, for example, makes the solution to the Negro problem depend on the speed with which Negroes accept and adopt white standards—is revealed in all kinds of striking ways, from Bobby Kennedy's assurance that a Negro can become President in forty years to the unfortunate tone of warm congratulation with which so many liberals address their Negro equals. It is the Negro, of course, who is presumed to have become equal—an achievement that not only proves the comforting fact that perseverance has no color but also overwhelmingly corroborates the white man's sense of his own value....

...There is absolutely no reason to suppose that white people are better equipped to frame the laws by which I am to be governed than I am. It is entirely unacceptable that I should have no voice in the political affairs of my own country, for I am not a ward of America; I am one of the first Americans to arrive on these shores.

This past, the Negro's past, of rope, fire, torture, castration, infanticide, rape; death and humiliation; fear by day and night, fear as deep as the marrow of the bone; doubt that he was worthy of life, since everyone around him denied it; sorrow for his women, for his kinfolk, for his children, who needed his protection, and whom he could not protect; rage, hatred, and murder, hatred for white men so deep that it often turned against him and his own, and made all love, all trust, all joy impossible—this past, this endless struggle to achieve and reveal and confirm a human identity, human authority, yet contains, for all its horror, something very beautiful....It demands great force and great cunning continually to assault the mighty and indifferent fortress of white supremacy, as Negroes in this country have done so long. If one is continually surviving the worst that life can bring, one eventually ceases to be controlled by a fear of what life can bring; whatever it brings must be borne....The apprehension of life here so briefly and inadequately sketched has been the experience of generations of Negroes, and it helps to explain how they have endured and how they have been able to produce children of kindergarten age who can walk through mobs to get to school....It demands great spiritual resilience not to hate the hater whose foot is on your neck, and an even greater miracle of perception and charity not to teach your child to hate....I have great respect for that unsung army of black men and women who trudged down back lanes and entered back doors, saying "Yes, sir" and "No, Ma'am" in order to acquire a new roof for the schoolhouse, new books, a new chemistry lab, more beds for the dormitories, more dormitories. They did not like saying "Yes, sir" and "No, Ma'am," but the country was in no hurry to educate Negroes, these black men and women knew that the job had to be done, and they put their pride in their pockets in order to do it.

...I could...see that the intransigence and ignorance of the white world might make...vengeance inevitable.... If we—and now I mean the relatively conscious whites and the relatively conscious blacks, who must, like lovers, insist on, or create, the consciousness of the others—do not falter in our duty now, we may be able, handful that we are, to end the racial nightmare, and achieve our country, and change the history of the world. If we do not now dare everything, the fulfillment of that prophesy, re-created from the Bible in song by a slave, is upon us: *God gave Noah the rainbow sign, No more water, the fire next time!*

Source: James Baldwin, *The Fire Next Time* (New York: The Dial Press, 1963), pp. 108-14, 119.

Black Power

During a civil rights march in 1966, Stokely Carmichael repeatedly chanted 'Black Power!" instead of the usual slogan "Freedom Now!" The media broadcast Carmichael's rallying cry. Blacks and whites alike demanded an explana:on or definition of "Black Power." Carmichael's clearest and most substantive definition came in a 1967 book he co-authored with Charles Hamilton entitled Black Power: The Politics of Liberation:

The adoption of the concept of Black Power is one of the most legitimate and healthy developments in American politics and race relations in our time.... It is a call for black people in this country to unite, to recognize their heritage, to build a sense of community. It is a call for black people to begin to define their own goals, to lead their own organizations and to support those organizations. It is a call to reject the racist institutions and values of this society.

The concept of Black Power rests on a fundamental premise: *Before a group can enter the open society, it must first close ranks.* By this we mean that group solidarity is necessary before a group can operate effectively from a bargaining position of strength in a pluralistic society. Traditionally, each new ethnic group in this society has found the route to social and political viability through the organization of its own institutions with which to represent its needs within the larger society. Studies in voting behavior specifically, and political behavior generally, have made it clear that politically the American pot has not melted. Italians vote for Rubino over O'Brien; Irish for Murphy over Goldberg, etc. This phenomenon may seem distasteful to some, but it has been and remains today a central fact of the American political system....

A white reporter set forth this point in other terms when he made the following observation about white Mississippi's manipulation of the anti-poverty program:..."Only when the Negro community can muster enough political, economic and professional strength to compete on somewhat equal terms, will Negroes believe in the possibility of true cooperation and whites accept its necessity. En route to integration, the Negro community needs to develop a greater independence—a chance to run its own affairs and not cave in whenever 'the man' barks."

The point is obvious: black people must lead and run their own organizations. Only black people can convey the revolutionary idea—and it is a revolutionary idea—that black people are able to do things themselves. Only they can help create in the community an aroused and continuing black consciousness that will provide the basis for political strength. In the past, white allies have often furthered white supremacy without the whites involved realizing it, or even wanting to do so. Black people must come together and do things for themselves. They must achieve self-identity and self-determination in order to have their daily needs met.

Black Power means, for example, that in Lowndes County, Alabama, a black sheriff can end police brutality. A black tax assessor and tax collector and county board of revenue can lay, collect, and channel tax moneys for the building of better roads and schools serving black people. In such areas as Lowndes, where black people have a majority, they will attempt to use power to exercise control. This is what they seek: control. When black people lack a majority, Black Power means proper representation and sharing of control. It means the creation of power bases, of strength, from which black people can press to change local or nation-wide patterns of oppression—instead of from weakness....

One of the tragedies of the struggle against racism is that up to this point there has been no national organization which could speak to the growing militancy of young black people in the urban ghettoes and the black-belt South. There has been only a "civil rights" movement, whose tone of voice was adapted to an audience of middle-class whites. It served as a sort of buffer zone between that audience and angry young blacks. It claimed to speak for the needs of a community, but it did not speak in the tone of that community. None of its so-called leaders could go into a rioting community and be listened to. In a sense, the blame must be shared—along with the mass media— by those leaders for what happened in Watts, Harlem, Chicago, Cleveland and other places. Each time the black people in those cities saw Dr. Martin Luther King get slapped they became angry. When they saw little black girls bombed to death in a *church* and civil rights workers ambushed and murdered, they were angrier; and when nothing happened, they were steaming mad. We had nothing to offer that they could see, except to go out and be beaten again. We helped to build their frustration....

According to its advocates, social justice will be accomplished by "integrating the Negro into the mainstream institutions of the society from which he has been traditionally excluded." This concept is based on the assumption that there is nothing of value in the black community and little of value could be created among black people. The thing to do is siphon off the "acceptable" black people into the surrounding middle-class white community.

The goals of integrationists are middle-class goals, articulated primarily by a small group of Negroes with middle-class aspirations or status.

Their kind of integration has meant that a few blacks "make it," leaving the black community, sapping it of leadership potential and know-how....[T]hose token Negroes—absorbed into a white mass—are of no value to the remaining black masses. They become meaningless show-pieces for a conscience-soothed white society. Such people will state that they would prefer to be treated "only as individuals, not as Negroes"; that they "are not and should not be preoccupied with race." This is a totally unrealistic position. In the first place, black people have not suffered as individuals but as members of a group; therefore, their liberation lies in group action.... Secondly, while color blindness may be a sound goal ultimately, we must realize that race is an overwhelming fact of life in this historical period. There is no black man in this country who can live "simply as a man." His blackness is an ever-present fact of this racist society, whether he recognizes it or not.

Source: Kwame Ture (formerly Stokely Carmichael) and Charles Hamilton, *Black Power: The Politics of Liberation* (New York: Vintage Books, 1992), pp. 44-46, 53-54.

Critics of Black Power

The NAACP continued to advocate a legal and reformist approach to civil rights. In the 1960s, some black activists criticized the NAACP's approach as outmoded and inadequate. Understandably, Roy Wilkins, who served as the NAACP's executive director from 1955 to 1977, was one of the first critics of the concept of "Black Power." He attacked "Black Power" in his address at the NAACP's 1966 convention:

...No matter how endlessly they try to explain it, the term "black power" means anti-white power. In a racially pluralistic society, the concept, the formation and the exercise of an ethnically tagged power means opposition to other ethnic powers, just as the term "white supremacy" means subjection of all non-white people. In the black-white relationship, it has to mean that every other ethnic power is the rival and the antagonist of "black power." It has to mean "going-it-alone." It has to mean separatism.

Now, separatism, whether on the rarefied debate level of "black power" or on the wishful level of a secessionist Freedom City in Watts, offers a disadvantaged minority little except the chance to shrivel and die.

The only possible dividend of "black power" is embodied in its offer to millions of frustrated and deprived and persecuted black people of a solace, a tremendous psychological lift, quite apart from its political and economic implications.

It is a reverse Mississippi, a reverse Hitler, a reverse Ku Klux Klan.

If these were evil in our judgment, what virtue can be claimed for black over white? If, as some proponents claim, this concept instills pride of race, cannot this pride be taught without preaching hatred or supremacy based upon race?

... Even if, through some miracle, it should be enthroned briefly in an isolated area, the human spirit, which knows no color or geography or time, would die a little, leaving for wiser and stronger and more compassionate men the painful beating back to the upward trail.

We of the NAACP will have none of this. We have fought it too long. It is the ranging of race against race on the irrelevant basis of skin color. It is the father of hatred and the mother of violence.

...We seek, therefore, as we have sought these many years, the inclusion of Negro Americans in the nation's life, not their exclusion. This is our land, as much so as it is any American's—every square foot of every city and town and village. The task of winning our share is not the easy one of disengagement and flight, but the hard one of work, of short as well as long jumps, of disappointments, and sweet successes....

Source: Dudley, pp. 231-33.

The National Urban League was founded in 1910 to help the thousands of blacks migrating to northern cities from the rural South. Whitney Young, Jr. became the League's director in October 1961. He outlined the League's strategy in the following essay:

The Urban League considers itself an action agency. Our action programs are designed to motivate youth to stay in school to get the best possible education; to expand the housing supply for the Negro population; to eliminate racial barriers in the employment and promotion of qualified Negroes; to strengthen Negro family life; and to stimulate self-help among Negro citizens in solving their problems.

It becomes clear that the strategy of the Urban League is twofold: (1) to help wipe out the last vestiges and barriers of discrimination and (2) to assist Negro citizens to rise through self-qualification until they can achieve the status of first-class citizenship not only in name but in fact. By working interracially, by obtaining the help of both the white and Negro community, by creating an atmosphere and climate of co-operation, and by emphasizing that it is in best interest of all to work together, the Urban League hopes to effect changes which would not otherwise be possible....

Source: Aptheker, pp. 357-58.

At the National Urban League Conference in 1963, Young posed the following challenge to the African American community:

> The Urban League is challenged, therefore, to see that the barriers of yesterday—the barriers built by prejudice, fear and indifference which are now crumbling—are not replaced by new barriers of apathy, of underdeveloped skills, of lack of training. If this happens, our gains will be but temporary, our victories hollow.
>
> Source: August Meier, Elliott Rudwick, and Francis L. Broderick, eds., *Black Protest Thought in the Twentieth Century*, 2nd edition (Indianapolis: Bobbs-Merrill Company, Inc., 1980), p. 327.

At its meeting in 1966, Young expressed his disgust at the attention that the media was giving to the "black power" controversy. He felt that it "diverted attention from the more meaningful debate around the real problems of poverty and discrimination." His thoughts were published in the August 5, 1966 issue of the New York Times:

> [We have] carefully refrained from becoming involved in the fruitless dispute over the value of a slogan which has not even yet been carefully defined by its originators.
>
> Rather we will continue to devote ourselves to bettering the position of the Negro in the nation.

We will continue through our unique structure to expand and develop positive programs of action which bring jobs to the unemployed, housing to the dispossessed, education to the deprived, and necessary voter education to the disenfranchised.

In the final analysis these are the things in our American system which bring power to both black and white citizens—and dignity and pride to all.

Source: Aptheker, pp. 437-38.

Black Panther Party

The Black Panther Party was a revolutionary organization based in Oakland, California. It was founded by two college-educated ghetto youths—Huey Newton and Bobby Seale. Its first aim was to protect blacks from police brutality from the almost all-white Oakland police force. Armed Panthers patrolled the city's streets, being nearby whenever a black person was pulled over by police. In time, the Party expanded its activities to include free breakfast programs for ghetto children. But the image of armed blacks in leather jackets captured the nation's attention and placed them on the FBI's most dangerous organizations list. The following manifesto (substantially edited for reasons of space limitations), drafted in 1966, became the central statement of the Black Panther Party's ideology:

1. We want freedom. We want power to determine the destiny of our Black Community.
2. We want full employment for our people.
3. We want an end to the robbery by the CAPITALIST of our Black Community.
4. We want decent housing, fit for shelter of human beings.
5. We want education for our people that exposes the true nature of this decadent American society. We want education that teaches us our true history and our role in the present-day society.
6. We want all black men to be exempt from military service.
7. We want an immediate end to POLICE BRUTALITY and MURDER of black people.
8. We want freedom for all black men held in federal, state, county and city prisons and jails.
9. We want all black people when brought to trial to be tried in court by a jury of their peer group or people from their black communities, as defined by the constitution of the United States.
10. We want land, bread, housing, education, clothing, justice and peace. And as our major political objective, a United Nations-supervised plebiscite to be held throughout the black colony in which only black colonial subjects will be allowed to participate, for the purpose of determining the will of black people as to their national destiny.

Source: Herb Boyd, *Black Panthers for Beginners* (New York: Writers and Readers Publishing, 1995), pp. 130-35.

Martin Luther King on Civil Rights and the Vietnam War

In 1967, King decided to speak out against the Vietnam War. This alienated King from moderate black leaders and the Johnson administration. Some accused him of distracting the civil rights movement from its primary task. In the following speech, King seems to answer his critics, excerpts from which follow:

For those who ask the question, "Aren't you a Civil Rights leader?" and thereby mean to exclude me from the movement for peace, I have this further answer. In 1957 when a group of us formed the Southern Christian Leadership Conference, we chose as our motto: "To save the soul of America." We were convinced that we could not limit our vision to certain rights for black people, but instead affirmed the conviction that America would never be free or saved from itself unless the descendants of its slaves were loosed completely from the shackles they still wear....

Now, it should be incandescently clear that no one who has any concern for the integrity and life of America today can ignore the present war. If America's soul becomes totally poisoned, part of the autopsy must read Vietnam. It can never be saved so long as it destroys the deepest hopes of men the world over.

As if the weight of such a commitment to the life and health of America were not enough, another burden of responsibility was placed upon me in 1964; and I cannot forget that the Nobel Prize for Peace was also a commission—a commission to work harder than I had ever worked before for the "brotherhood of man." This is a calling that takes me beyond national allegiances, but even if it were not present I would yet have to live with the meaning of my commitment to the ministry of Jesus Christ. To me the relationship of this ministry to the making of peace is so obvious that I sometimes marvel at those who ask me why I am speaking against the war. Could it be that they do not know that the good news was meant for all men—for Communist and capitalist, for their children and ours, for black and for white, for revolutionary and conservative? Have they forgotten that my ministry is in obedience to the one who loved his enemies so fully that he died for them? What then can I say to the "Viet Cong" or to Castro or to Mao as a faithful minister of this one? Can I threaten them with death, or must I not share with them my life?...

And as I ponder the madness of Vietnam and search within myself for ways to understand and respond to compassion my mind goes constantly to the people of that peninsula. They must see

Americans as strange liberators. The Vietnamese proclaimed their own independence in 1945 after a combined French and Japanese occupation, and before the communist revolution in China....Even though they quoted the American Declaration of Independence in their own document of freedom, we refused to recognize them. Instead, we decided to support France in its re-conquest of her former colony....

Source: Aptheker, pp. 482-83.

Poor People's Campaign

King felt that radical economic measures were necessary to solve the growing violence in the United States. His views were published in Look *magazine eight days after his assassination on April 4, 1968:*

The policy of the federal government is to play Russian roulette with riots; it is prepared to gamble with another summer of disaster. Despite two consecutive summers of violence, not a single basic cause of riots has been corrected. All of the misery that stoked the flames of rage and rebellion remains undiminished. With unemployment, intolerable housing, and discriminatory education a scourge in Negro ghettos, Congress and the administration still tinker with trivial, halfhearted measures....

...The fact is inescapable that the tactic of nonviolence, which had then dominated the thinking of the civil rights movement, has in the last two years not been playing its transforming role. Nonviolence was a creative doctrine in the South because it checkmated the rabid segregationists who were thirsting for an opportunity to physically crush Negroes. Nonviolent direct action enabled the Negro to take to the streets in active protest, but it muzzled the guns of the oppressor because even he could not shoot down in daylight unarmed men, women, and children. This is the reason there was less loss of life in ten years of southern protests than in ten days of northern riots.

Today, the northern cities have taken on the conditions we faced in the South. Police, national guard, and other armed bodies are feverishly preparing for repression. They can be curbed not by unorganized resort to force by desperate Negroes but only by a massive wave of militant nonviolence. Nonviolence was never more relevant or as effective than today for the North. It also may be the instrument of our national salvation....

The time has come for a return to mass nonviolent protest. Accordingly, we are planning a series of such demonstrations this spring and summer, to begin in Washington, D.C. They will have Negro and white participation, and they will seek to benefit the poor of both races....

We call our demonstration a campaign for jobs and income because we feel that the economic question is the most crucial that black people, and poor people generally, are confronting. There is a literal depression in the Negro community. When you have mass unemployment in the Negro community, it's called a social problem; when you have mass unemployment in the white community, it's called a depression. The fact is, there is a major depression in the Negro community. The unemployment rate is extremely high, and among Negro youth, it goes up as high as forty percent in some cities.

We need an economic bill of rights. This would guarantee a job to all people who want to work and are able to work. It would also guarantee an income for all who are not able to work. Some people are too young, some are too old, some are physically disabled, and yet in order to live, they need income. It would mean creating certain public-service jobs, but that could be done in a few weeks. A program that would really deal with jobs could minimize—I don't say stop—the number of riots that could take place this summer.

Our whole campaign, therefore, will center on the job question, with other demands, like housing, that are closely tied to it. We feel that much more building of housing for low-income people should be done. On the educational front, the ghetto schools are in bad shape in terms of quality, and we feel that a program should be developed to spend at least a thousand dollars per pupil. Often, they are so far behind that they need more and special attention, the best quality education that can be given....

I'm committed to nonviolence....I have found it to be a philosophy of life that regulates not only my dealings in the struggle for racial justice but also my dealings with people, with my own self....

But I'm frank enough to admit that if our nonviolent campaign doesn't generate some progress, people are just going to engage in more violent activity, and the discussion of guerrilla warfare will be more extensive.

Source: Aptheker, pp. 545-46, 548-51.

Epilogue

When Martin Luther King, Jr. gave his "I have a dream" speech at the Lincoln Memorial in 1963, it seemed as if the African American community spoke in a single voice. By 1967, however, it was clear that no such unity existed. Some black organizations, such as the SCLC, the NAACP and the National Urban League, continued their strategy of achieving equality and integration through legislation, court decisions and individual efforts of diligent blacks. But other organizations, such as The Nation of Islam, the Black Panthers and the (later) SNCC, called for blacks to seek independence from white society, by violence if necessary. By this time, King's own focus was changing. He realized that the problems of northern blacks were more economic than legal. No segregation laws existed in the North. But northern blacks lived in cities with growing unemployment, declining public services, decaying infrastructures and rising crime rates.

At the end of 1967, King decided to launch a campaign to make the nation aware of the plight of its poor citizens. The "Poor People's Campaign" would bring impoverished people of all races and color—blacks, whites, Mexican Americans, Native Americans—to Washington, D.C. King hoped the demonstration would pressure President Johnson to increase the funding of his "War on Poverty." King had lost much of his support from moderate black leaders and the white liberal establishment when he came out in opposition of the Vietnam War. His Poor People's Campaign did not have much support from Black Power advocates, who considered him too cautious and conciliatory. King was visibly depressed over the prospects of the upcoming Campaign. In early April of 1968, King received a request from striking garbage workers in Memphis, Tennessee to come and support their effort. King agreed to go because the strike for fair wages and better working conditions lay at the heart of his new direction.

On April 3, King spoke at a mass meeting in Memphis. King told the audience that "we've got some difficult times ahead." He nevertheless had a vision that African Americans would "get to the promised land" someday. King said that he may not be with them when they did. This proved to be prophetic. King was shot dead on the balcony of his motel the following day. His assassination set off a wave of urban racial violence. The Poor People's Campaign continued after King's death. But it failed to generate broad national support or change national policies toward the poor.

Four decades after King's death, the impact of the civil rights movement remains uncertain. Blacks have made substantial gains in education and income. The proportion of blacks with four years of high school education increased from less than 10 percent in the 1950s to over 75 percent in the 1990s. The number of black professionals has increased exponentially since the 1950s. All laws mandating racial segregation have been eliminated. Laws have been enacted

119

which prohibit employers and public accommodations from discriminating on the basis of race or color. However, predominantly black schools in the inner-cities are deteriorating. The unemployment rate among black teens is substantially higher than that of their white counterparts. Many black professionals feel that "a glass ceiling" keeps them from attaining the highest positions in America's corporations. Blacks make up a disproportionately high ratio of the nation's prison and death row populations. Most disturbing is the fact that the majority of Americans feel race relations have deteriorated since the 1960s. Has America overcome its problems of race and color? It may someday. But for now, the struggle continues for those seeking racial justice.

Time Line

1954 Brown v. Board of Education overturns the "separate but equal" doctrine of Plessy v. Ferguson (1896).

1955 Rosa Parks refuses to give up her seat, setting off the Montgomery bus boycott.

1957 President Eisenhower calls in federal troops to enforce the integration of Central High School in Little Rock, Arkansas.

1960 Black students launch the "sit-in" movement to desegregate public facilities.

1961 Freedom Riders attempt to desegregate the South's transportation facilities.

1962 Efforts to desegregate facilities in Albany, Georgia fail.

1962 James Meredith attempts to attend the University of Mississippi.

1963 The brutal suppression of efforts to desegregate Birmingham, Alabama by police commissioner "Bull" Connor is televised nationally.

1963 Governor Wallace tries to block the admission of black students to the University of Alabama.

1963 Medgar Evers, the NAACP's field secretary in Mississippi, is murdered.

1963 The March on Washington is climaxed by King's "I have a dream" speech.

1964 Malcolm X leaves the Nation of Islam and forms his own temple.

1964 The "Freedom Summer Project" employs white college students from outside the South to register black voters in Mississippi.

1964 The Mississippi Freedom Democratic Party is formed. Its delegates challenge the seating of the state's all-white delegation at the Democratic National Convention.

1964 Civil Rights Act outlaws racial discrimination in public accommodations.

1964 King wins the Nobel Peace Prize.

1965 Civil rights marchers are attacked by Selma police at Edmund Pettus Bridge.

1965 Voting Rights Act facilitates federal intervention to insure black voting rights.

1965 Malcolm X is assassinated.

1965 Riot in Watts, California leaves 34 dead, 900 injured, and 3,500 arrested.

1965 "Black power" advocate Stokely Carmichael replaces John Lewis as chairperson of SNCC.

1965   Civil rights demonstrators are stoned by white residents of Chicago.

1965   The Black Panther Party is founded in Oakland, California by Huey Newton and Bobby Seale.

1967   King announces his opposition to the War in Vietnam.

1967   Race riots break out in Newark, Detroit, New York, Cleveland, Chicago, Atlanta and Washington, D.C.

1968   King is assassinated while supporting striking garbage workers in Memphis, Tennessee.

1968   The Poor People's Campaign erects "Resurrection City" in Washington, D.C.

Suggested Further Reading

Abraham, Henry. *Freedom and the Court: Civil Rights and Liberties in the United States,* Second Edition. New York: Oxford University Press, 1972.

Branch, Taylor. *Parting the Waters: America in the King Years, 1954-63.* New York: Touchstone Book, 1988.

_____ . *Pillar of Fire: America in the King Years, 1963-65.* New York: Simon & Schuster, 1998.

Carawan, Guy and Candie, eds. *Sing for Freedom: The Story of the Civil Rights Movement through its Songs.* . Bethlehem: Sing Out Publication, 1992.

Carson, Clayborne, David Garrow, Gerald Gill, Vincent Harding, Darlene Clark Hine, eds. *Eyes on the Prize Civil Rights Reader: Documents, Speeches and First hand Accounts from the Black Freedom Struggle, 1954-1990.* New York: Penguin, 1991.

Eagles, Charles, ed. *The Civil Rights Movement in America.* Jackson: University Press of Mississippi, 1986.

Ficter, Joseph, "American Religion and the Negro," in Talcott Parsons and Kenneth Clark, eds. *The Negro American.* Boston: Houghton Mifflin, 1966.

Frazier, Thomas, ed. *Afro-American History: Primary Sources.* New York: Harcourt, Bace & World, 1970.

Grant, Joanne, ed. *Black Protest: History, Documents, and Analyses, 1619 to Present*. New York: Fawcett Premier, 1968.

Hamilton, Charles. *The Black Preacher in America*. New York: William Morrow, 1972.

Hoobler, Dorothy and Thomas. *The African American Family Album*. New York: Oxford University Press, 1995.

Hughes, Langston, Milton Meltzer and C. Eric Lincoln. *A Pictorial History of Blackamericans*. New York: Crown Publishers, 1983.

King, Martin Luther, Jr. *Stride Toward Freedom*. New York: Harper & Row, 1958.

Lerner, Gerda, ed. *Black Women in White America: A Documentary History*. New York: Vintage Books, 1972.

Malcolm X, with assistance of Alex Haley. *The Autobiography of Malcolm X*. New York: Grove Press, 1966.

McMillen, Neil. *The Citizen's Council: Organized Resistance to the Second Reconstruction, 1954-64*. Urbana: University of Illinois Press, 1971.

Meier, August and Elliot Rudwick, eds. *Black Protest in the Sixties*. Chicago: Quadrangle Books, 1970.

Namorato, Michael, ed. *Have We Overcome? Race Relations Since Brown.* Jackson: University Press of Mississippi, 1979.

Riley, Winbush, ed. *My Soul Looks Back, 'Less I Forget: A Collection of Quotations by People of Color.* New York: Harper Perennial, 1993.

Sarratt, Reed. *The Ordeal of Desegregation: The First Decade.* New York: Harper & Row, 1966.

Sitkoff, Harvard. *The Struggle for Black Equality, 1954-1992.* Revised Edition, New York: Hill & Wang, 1993.

Weisbrot, Robert. *Freedom Bound: A History of America's Civil Rights Movement.* New York: Plume, 1991.

Young, Whitney, Jr. *To Be Equal.* New York: McGraw-Hill, 1964.